AF018

MASSIMILIANO AFIERO

AXIS FORCES 18

WW2 AXIS FORCES

The Axis Forces 018 - First edition July 2021by Luca Cristini Editor for the brand Soldiershop
Cover & Art Design by soldiershop factory. ISBN code: 978-88-93277761

The Axis Forces number 18 – July 2021

Direction and editing: **Via San Giorgio, 11 – 80021 AFRAGOLA (NA) -ITALY**

Managing and Chief Editor: Massimiliano Afiero

Email: maxafiero@libero.it - **Website**: www.maxafiero.it

Contributors

Tomasz Borowski, Grégory Bouysse, Stefano Canavassi, Carlos Caballero Jurado, Rene Chavez, Gary Costello, Paolo Crippa, Carlo Cucut, Antonio Guerra, Lars Larsen, Christophe Leguérandais, Eduardo M. Gil Martínez, Michael D. Miller, Peter Mooney, Marc Rikmenspoel, Hugh Page Taylor, Charles Trang, Cesare Veronesi, Sergio Volpe

Editorial

Eighty years ago, exactly in the summer of 1941, on June 22, 1941, German military forces invaded the Soviet Union, beginning one of the largest military campaigns of the entire Second World War. A premeditated action, planned for some time, but which took European and world diplomacy by surprise, considering that in August 1939, Stalin and Hitler had signed an agreement to define their spheres of influence on the European continent, the so-called Ribbentrop-Molotov Pact. To invade the Soviet territory, alongside the Germans, numerous foreign contingents also participated, from countries the allied with Germany, such as Finland, Hungary, Romania, Slovakia and subsequently also Italy and Spain, not to forget then the numerous foreign voluntary units organized by the Germans in the occupied countries: France, Denmark, Norway, Holland, Belgium. German propaganda was able to transform the military invasion into a real 'Crusade against Bolshevism', against the Stalinist regime, accused of wanting in turn to invade the European continent. From the October Revolution of 1917, a tyrant state had arisen which from its inception adopted a policy of terror and violence to impose its power. The very birth of the fascist movements throughout Europe was due precisely to this desire to be able to restrain the Bolsheviks in their attempt to expand the Red terror throughout the European continent, from the end of the Great War to the beginning of the Second World War. Thanks to the alliance with Hitler, Stalin took the opportunity to invade part of Poland itself, Finland, the Baltic Republics, the Romanian regions of Bukovina and Bessarabia and would never stop. Hitler thus anticipated his moves, being the first to invade Soviet Russia. Naturally we will start from this issue of the magazine to retrace the fundamental stages of the war on the Eastern front, dealing, as always, mainly with foreign voluntary units. Let's now analyze the contents of this new issue of the magazine. Let's start with the history of the Walloon Legion on the Eastern front, we continue with the second part of the history of the Frikorps Danmark, with the use of the Nord Division in the summer of 1941 on the Finnish front and finally we close with an article dedicated to the insignia used by the Italian volunteers in the Waffen-SS. Happy reading everyone and see you at the next issue.

Massimiliano Afiero

Contents

WALLONIE

Walloon volunteers in the German armed forces

By Massimiliano Afiero

In Belgium occupied by the German armed forces in May 1940, there were always two peoples, different in religion and language, the Walloons in the south, Catholic and French-speaking and the Flemish in the north, Protestant and German-speaking. For obvious racial reasons, the Germans immediately accepted Flemish volunteers into their ranks in their *Waffen-SS* formations since 1940, in the *Westland, Nordwest* regiments and also establishing a Germanic *Allgemeine-SS* unit in Flanders. With the Walloons, however, the collaboration only came later, thanks above all to the action of Léon Degrelle.

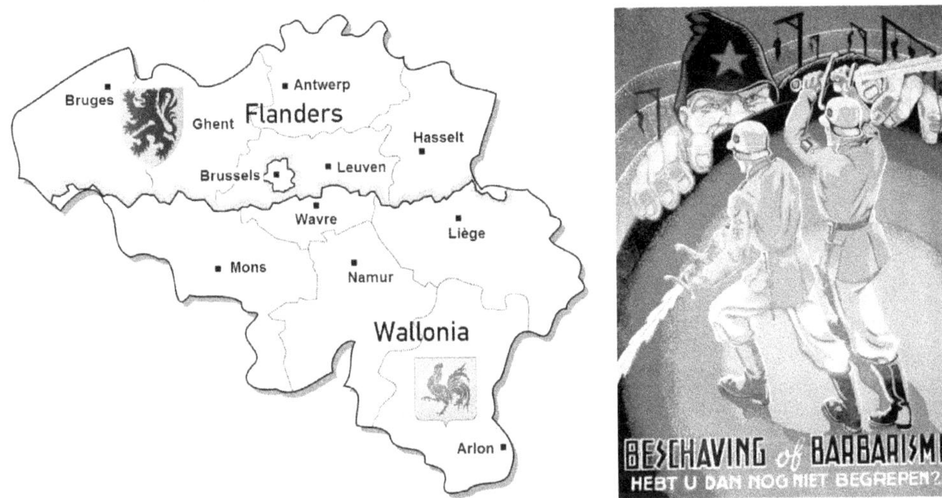

Left, Flanders and Wallonia. Right, Flemish and Walloon propaganda poster: ***'Civilization or barbarism. Do you still not understand?'.***

Léon Degrelle.

In the aftermath of the *Barbarossa* operation, the formation of two voluntary legions began in Belgium, a Flemish, organizated by the *Waffen-SS* and a Walloon, organizated by the German army (*Heer*).

The fascist movements in Wallonia

The fascist revolutionary wave in Europe naturally also affected Belgium, where the rivalry between the two Flemish and Walloon ethnic groups gave rise to numerous nationalist and independence political groups. On the Walloon side, the key personality of Belgian fascism was certainly that of Léon Degrelle[1]. The first Belgian fascist movement had already been founded in May 1922, the *Légion Nationale,*

Brussels, August 1941: Degrelle, with the uniform of the Formations de Combat before leaving for the front.

Palais des Arts at Brussels, August 1941: Degrelle speacking before the departure of the volunteers.

Degrelle, Fernand Rouleau, and Victor Matthys (behind Degrelle) leaving the Palais des Arts at Brussels.

a far-right movement led by Paul Hoornaert. The movement later absorbed other small nationalist groups such as the *Fasceau Belge* and the *Jeunesses Nationales*. Degrelle initially remained out of these early fascist-inspired political groupings and also later refused their collaboration. In 1929, Louvain's Catholic Action entrusted him with the direction of a small publishing house, the *Christus Rex* (Christ the King), which Degrelle transformed into a weapon to spread his Catholic-inspired fascism. In 1932, Degrelle began publishing a new magazine, REX, which enjoyed unprecedented success across the country. On November 2, 1935, Degrelle founded the *Parti Populaire de Rex*, which in 1936 obtained 34 seats in the senate. *Rexism* was fighting for a vast work of social reforms, for a series of measures aimed at restoring the image of the Christian family, for a new Europe against great finance and Bolshevism, but above all it was fighting for the unity of the country, divided between Flemish and Walloons. In the years immediately preceding the outbreak of the Second World War, Degrelle's party maintained a pacifist attitude, tending to want to leave Belgium out of the war and away from the Franco-English alliance. This political line was misunderstood as a form of support, albeit indirect, to the German expansion policy, which is why at the beginning of the

Degrelle leads the column of volunteers leaving for the front on the streets of Brussels.

Degrelle in Rexist party uniform and German officers at the Brussels railway station.

German offensive on the western front in May 1940, Degrelle and his followers became the subject of indiscriminate persecution from part of the Belgian government until he was arrested for alleged subversive activity. Degrelle was transferred first to Brussels, then to Bruges and finally to Dunkirk, where he was handed over to the French who in turn transferred him from prison to prison. Degrelle miraculously escaped the Abbeville massacre in France, where around twenty Belgian prisoners (including three women, a priest and Joris Van Severen head of the Flemish Verdinaso movement), were shot in retaliation by French soldiers, charged with being spies. With the armistice, on July 22, 1940, Degrelle was freed from the Vernet concentration camp in France, but the German authorities remained uninterested in his Rex party. Degrelle then resumed publishing his newspaper, *Le Pays Réel*. In the same month of July 1940, the General Council of the Rexist Movement started the formation of a new paramilitary unit on the model of the German SS, the *Formations de Combat*. The scope of this unit was to protect the movement's leaders and assemblies and to collaborate with the local police and German authorities to maintain order in the country. At the end of the year, his strength came to count about 4,000 staff. The members of the *Formations de Combat* wore a dark blue uniform and carried on their right pocket a black shield with red Burgundian Cross. Rutger Simoens was chosen as the first commander of the unit, later replaced in February 1941 by Fernand Rouleau. On January 5, 1941, a large demonstration of the rexists in Liège was organized, attended by about

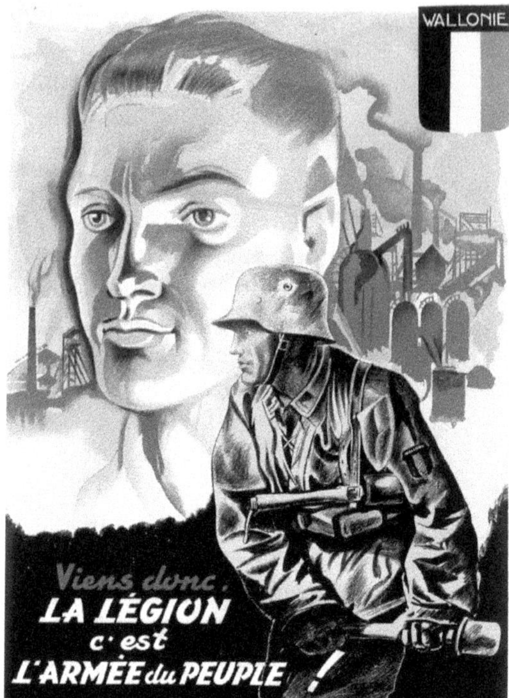

Poster to encourage recruitement in the Walloon Legion, Summer 1941.

Wallonie Volunteer Legion Arm-Shield (*Rene Chavez Collection*).

five thousand people. Degrelle ended his speech with a *'Heil Hitler'*, attesting his alignment with the National Socialism. Of course, this declared loyalty to the *Führer* created many problems for him within the party, but at the same time attracted the attention of the Germans, who until then had been reluctant to cooperate with the French-speaking part of Belgium.

The Walloon Legion

When Operation *Barbarossa* began in June 1941, Léon Degrelle returned to the political scene, to actively participate in the crusade against Bolshevism: in Brussels, the *Kommandostab Z*, a special section of the *Militärverwaltung,* the German military occupation authority, under command of *Hauptmann* Baumann made contact with Fernand Rouleau, head of the *Formations de Combat* to begin the formation of a Walloon unit to be sent to the Eastern front. After receiving the authorization, the official announcement was made by Degrelle himself on July 6, 1941, in Brussels. Across Wallonia, the Rexists embarked on a frantic recruiting campaign: in less than a week, more than a thousand volunteers showed up and passed the medical examination. The volunteers came from all social classes with a good number of students. Most of the volunteers were members of the Formations de Combat, others came from the *AGRA, Les Amis du Grand Reich Allemand,* another pro-German nationalist group. In addition, there were also a dozen Russians exiled to Belgium after the Bolshevik revolution. Of course, Léon Degrelle himself was one of the first volunteers and

Walloon volunteers in training at Meseritz camp, summer 1941 (*Dernier Carré – Léon Degrelle*).

Léon Degrelle in German uniform. Note the Walloon arm schield.

publicly announced it during a demonstration organized in Liège on 20 July 1941. The German authorities immediately granted him the rank of *lieutenant*, but Degrelle refused, preferring to start his military career in the German army, as a simple private soldier. According to order no. 3680/41 of the German Command, the Walloon volunteers were officially placed in the *Wallonisches Infanterie Bataillon Nr. 373* and transferred to the training camp of Meseritz, near the Polish border. On August 8, 1941, 860 Walloon volunteers left Brussels station. Before leaving, a large demonstration was organized in Brussels, first at the Palace of Fine Arts and then on the Royal Square, in front of the statue of Geoffrey du Boulogne, the inspirer of the first crusade against the infidels. On August 12, 1941, the volunteers arrived in Meseritz, immediately starting basic military training. On August 25, the Walloons swore an oath of allegiance to Hitler in the fight against Bolshevism. *Major* Georges Jacobs, an officer of the Belgian colonial troops, was placed in command of the Legion. *Oberleutnant* Lucien Lippert was appointed as a staff officer and Dr. Pierre Jacquemin as the medical officer. To offer religious services was the chaplain George Sales of the abbey of Clervaux. The Walloons were provided with army uniforms. A German made arm shield showing the Belgian national colors, with black, yellow, red vertical stripes, under the word *'Wallonie'*

Walloon volunteers with the Legion flag with the Burgundy cross, September 1941 (NARA).

***Hauptmann* George Tchekhoff (*Dernier Carré – Léon Degrelle*).**

in yellow on a black panel, was worn on their uniforms. The 373rd Walloon Infantry Battalion was organized into four companies, three rifle and one machine gun, under the orders of the following commanders:

1.Kompanie: Hauptmann Albert Van Damme

2.Kompanie: Hauptmann Willy Heyvaert

3.Kompanie: Hauptmann Georges Tchekhoff

4.Kompanie: Hauptmann René Dupré

Leutnant Leppin was assigned to the Walloon legion, as a German liaison officer. Lèon Degrelle served as a simple soldier in the first platoon of the first company of the *Hauptmann* Van Damme.

Degrelle and Walloon volunteers on the Eastern Front, Autumn 1941.

On the Eastern front

Légion Wallonie left Meseritz camp on October 16, 1941. On November 2, 1941, the journey ended in Dnepropetrovsk. The Burgundians arrived in Ukraine, just when the march of the German forces had temporarily stopped due to the abundant autumn rains that had transformed the landscape into an immense quagmire. After a few days of rest, in the morning of November 6, in pouring rain, the Walloons crossed the Dnieper river, continuing towards Novo-Moscova, about thirty kilometers further east. A few days of rest were granted to the legion by the German command, but at the same time, the unit had to ensure control of some positions and send patrols to explore and remove the threat from the partisan units. From mid-November, the various Legion units were temporarily dispersed to be engaged on a security mission in the rear on the Donetz front. On November 26, a new marching order came to the front lines, with cold and snow. The villages of Petropavloka, Merchevaja and Slavianka were crossed. Due to bad weather conditions, the connections between the various companies were interrupted. And so, on December 1, 1941, the *Hauptmann* Tchekhoff arrived in Grichino-Selo, with only two scouts from his company.

Movements of the Walloon units between November 1941 and February 1942.

The machine gunner Léon Degrelle at Tscherbinovka, Christmas 1941.

Léon Degrelle with *Hauptmann* Pierre Pauly, the new commander of the Legion.

Shortly thereafter, his aide, Pierre Dengis, arrived with bad news. *Hauptmann* René Dupré, commander of the fourth company, was killed when he stepped on a mine. It was the first death in the Legion. The march resumed on December 5, passing through the towns of Novo-Ekonomitcheskoïe, Alexandrovka and Kostantinovka. On December 10, 1941, the Legion was attached to the *101.leichte-Infanterie-Division*, under the orders of the *General der Artillerie* Erich Marcks, in turn subordinate to the *III.Armee-Korps*. The terrible weather conditions, inadequate training and the lack of winter equipment, helped to decimate the Legion. The older members, about fifty in all, were demobilized and repatriated in a pitiful conditions. In the meantime, the *Wallonie* Legion had moved to Tcherbinovka, where it established its positions for the winter and where the legionaries spent Christmas. The legionaries settled in the buildings of the local school. Placed in reserve, the Legion had shrunk to about five hundred men still able to fight. Until Christmas, the legionnaires continued to be engaged in security tasks in the rear, but above all they had to fight against the cold

New unit commanders

After the death of the *Hauptmann* Dupré, all the company commanders, with the exception of Tchekhoff in the third, changed. *Leutnant* Alfred Lisein assumed command of the first, *Leutnant* Joseph Daulne of the second and *Oberleutnant* Arthur Buydts of the fourth. *Hauptmann* Jacobs, deemed unable to conduct a military unit in the field, was replaced by the former Belgian Army officer, *Hauptmann* Pierre Pauly. The German liaison officer *Leutnant* Leppin was also

Oberleutnant Lucien Lippert.

Walloon volunteers on the march, 1942.

dismissed at the explicit request of Degrelle. In his place came the *Hauptmann* Erich von Lehe, a reserve officer.

Legion order of battle January 1942

Commander: *Hauptmann* Pierre Pauly
Staff: *Oberleutnant* Lucien Lippert, *Leutnant* Thys
Medical service: *Oberleutnant* Dr. Silvère Miesse, *Leutnant* Dr. Albert
German liaison officer: *Hauptmann* Dr. Erich von Lehe
1.Kompanie: *Leutnant* Alfred Lisein
2.Kompanie: *Leutnant* Joseph Daulne
3.Kompanie: *Hauptmann* Georges Tchekhoff
4.Kompanie: *Oberleutnant* Arthur Buydts

In mid-January, the strength of the Battalion due to illness and cold dropped to about 320 legionnaires. The Walloon units were to be integrated into the *Kampfgruppe Tröger,* including the *I./SS-Inf.Rgt. 'Germania'* of the *Wiking* division, a Croatian infantry battalion, a reconnaissance company, a dozen tanks, a 105mm artillery group and a 75mm battery. On January 26, 1942, the *Wallonie* Legion left Tscherbinovka to go first to Ekonomitcheskoïe and from here to Grischino, where the units were loaded onto a train to reach the village of Rosa-Luxemburg in early February, passing under the control of the *100.leichte Infanterie-Division* of *Generalleutnant* Werner Sanne. On 11 February 1942, for merit in the field, Léon Degrelle was promoted to the rank of *Gefreiter* (corporal).

Gromowaja-Balka

On February 17, 1942, the *Kampfgruppe Tröger* was transferred to the Stepanovka area to reinforce the positions of General Sanne's *100.leichte Infanterie-Division.* Reunited, the Wallonie legion was ordered to occupy the village of Gromowaja-Balka, about eight kilometers north of the Samara River. The village of Gromowaja-Balka was located on the banks of a stream at the bottom of a valley: Commander Pauly immediately distributed his units. The first company of *Leutnant* Lisein was placed in defense of the north-western part, the third of *Hauptmann* Tchekhoff the western part, with an isolated foothold

An *MG-34* on a defensive position, February 1942.

A German *Pak 37mm* engaged against Soviet tanks.

A desperate counterattack was launched....

defended by the Ruelle platoon five hundred meters further away. The second of *Leutnant* Daulne, occupied the isbas (*izba*) located to the north. The southeastern part was assigned to the fourth company of *Leutnant* Buydts. Soviet artillery began to hit the village. A few days later, the company commanders received orders to launch patrols in advance to try to assess the strength and positions of enemy forces in the sector. After ten days, without having fought, the Legion had already lost nine killed and forty-five wounded. The actual fighters had dropped to around 500 men. At dawn on February 28, 1942, the Soviets attacked the position: two Soviet regiments, almost six thousand soldiers supported by an armored formation of fourteen tanks, launched themselves into the assault. A real flood of fire hit the Wallonie's positions. The 37mm pieces of the Croats and the 80mm mortars of the Walloons came into action immediately. The first shots went short, then the elevation was adjusted and the attackers began to suffer losses. However, the Soviet infantry masses continued to advance. In their foxholes, Walloon machine-gunners and riflemen had been ordered to open fire only at the last moment. When the Soviet infantrymen arrived at about fifty meters from their positions, the Walloons opened fire creating wide openings among the Soviet infantry. Furious close-quartier combat followed in the village, where each isba was lost

Léon Degrelle and the commander of the Legion *Hauptmann* Pierre Pauly, engaged in combat in Gromowaja-Balka.

An *MG-34* firing against Soviet Infantry, February 1942.

and reconquered several times. Some elements of the *Wiking Germania* regiment that survived the battle of Otcheterino arrived in reinforcement. The Walloons continued to resist all enemy assaults, but suffering heavy losses. The German artillery fire also intervened in support, the batteries of which were further back. To try to overcome the resistance of the Walloons and avoid the minefields north of the village, the Soviets launched themselves in a vast movement circumventing from the west, investing the positions of the second company of *Leutnant* Daulne, located in the north, reinforced by a platoon of the company machine gunners under the orders of the *Oberfeldwebel* Bosquion. When the situation became critical, the Closset platoon of the first company also intervened. A desperate counterattack was launched with all the men available, then the volunteers retreated south of the valley. A Soviet flamethrower tank entered the village, setting all the isbas on fire, one after the other. New fighting followed in the midst of the flames. The Soviet infantry continued to hit the village, the Walloons opened fire with all their weapons. The fighting continued isba by isba. Blasts and explosions followed one another with a hellish rhythm. At around 8:30 in the morning, the first company of the *Leutnant* Lisein found itself attacked from the rear due to the withdrawal of the second company and therefore was forced to withdraw. To try to

A defensive position with an *MG-34.*

A Soviet tank destroyed, February 1942.

A squadron of *Stukas* came to support....

stem the strong enemy pressure, commander Pauly ordered some counterattacks, thanks to which the Walloons managed to regain some isbas, and then immediately afterwards were driven back to the center of the village. The positions had to be held, since there was no natural obstacle behind them, only a completely frozen plain. At around 11:00 in the morning, the defenders of Gromowaja-Balka had to fall back again, leaving other isbas in the hands of the enemy. Towards midday, *Hauptmann* Pauly was forced to move the command post of the battalion, which risked being overrun at any moment. Three quarters of Gromowaja-Balka were now in the hands of the Soviets. *Hauptmann* Pauly ordered a new counterattack, leading it personally: the legionaries advanced from isba to isba, running, firing and shouting. The first company regained its positions again. In the afternoon, while the Soviets were preparing for a new assault on the village, a squadron of *Stukas* came to support. Bombs dropped by dive bombers exploded amid the masses of infantry and wagons grouped on the outskirts of Gromowaja-Balka. A few German tanks arrived soon after, along with infantry units. The Walloon legionaries launched a final and daring counterattack, during which Léon Degrelle distinguished himself. With a formidable impetus, the legionaries retook the ruins of the village. After passing the last isbas, they launched themselves in pursuit of the Soviets who were retreating in disorder, taking numerous prisoners. At the end of the battle, *Hauptmann* Pauly promoted Degrelle to *Oberfeldwebel* on the field, for the courage shown in combat. The defense of Gromowaja-Balka cost the legion 65 dead and 110 wounded. On the evening of March 4, the legionaries were directed

March 2, 1942: Degrelle receives the Iron Cross Second Class from General Werner Otto Sanne in the presence of the Legion commander, *Hauptmann* Pauly.

Spring 1942: *Leutnant* Degrelle with other Walloon volunteers in a Ukrainian village.

to the village of Blagodatch, where on March 13, 1942, General Sanne delivered thirty-seven Second-Class Iron Crosses to the Walloons.

Reorganization

Due to the severe losses suffered and the lack of personnel, Commander Pauly decided to dissolve the second company, assigning his survivors to the other companies. In command of the first company, *Oberfeldwebel* Jules Mathieu took over, in command of the third, *Oberfeldwebel* Ruelle and in command of the machine gun company, *Leutnant* Daulne. *Hauptmann* Pauly was repatriated, officially for 'health reasons'. On April 6, 1942, *Hauptmann* Tchekhoff, an officer of Caucasian origin, who had served in the Czarist imperial navy until the revolution, took his place. Léon Degrelle was appointed ordinance officer, which allowed him to work closely with the Legion staff. On May 1, 1942, Degrelle was promoted to *Leutnant* for distinguishing himself in combat and on May 21, 1942 he was decorated with the Iron Cross First Class. Between April and early May, the Legion was assigned as a reserve unit for the *68.Infanterie-Division.*

Legion Order of battle May 1942

Commander: *Hauptmann* Georges Tchekhoff (until June 4, 1942)

Spring 1942, from the left *Hauptmann* von Lehe, Léon Degrelle and *Hauptmann* Pauly.

Léon Degrelle and General Ernst Rupp, Spring 1942.

From the left, Degrelle, von Lehe and Tchekhoff.

Adjutant: *Oberleutnant* Lucien Lippert
German liaison officer: *Hptm.* Dietzl
1.Kompanie: *Leutnant* Jules Mathieu
2.Kompanie: *Leutnant* Georges Ruelle
3.Kompanie: *Leutnant* C. Bosquion
Pioneer platoon: *Obfwbl* Mirgain

Donetz Front

While the Legion's service units were grouped in Velikoïepole, the infantry companies marched towards Alexandrovka. The Walloon Legion had been transferred to the *97.Jäger Division*, under the orders of General Ernst Rupp. With the start of the summer, the German high command had decided to resume the offensive on the Eastern front.

The objectives of the new offensive, assigned to the Army Group South, defined by Hitler in directive number 41 of 5 April 1942, codenamed *'Fall Blau'* (Plan Blue), were: the annihilation of the Soviet forces located between the Donetz basin and the Don, the conquest of the Caucasian passes and the possession of the rich oil fields on the Caspian Sea. In preparation for the new offensive, the Walloon volunteers were to be part of the troops intended to reduce the Soviet bridgehead formed during the winter in the Izjum-Barvenkovo-Slaviansk region and to drive the enemy north of the Donetz River. To this end, on May 6, 1942, the Walloon legion reached Varvarovka. From here, groups of volunteers were sent immediately to go and take over the German troops who occupied the ridge in front of Jablenskaïa, a village occupied by the Soviets. At dawn, the Burgundians discovered their new sector: in front of them stretched a field of mines, protected by barbed wire. A hundred yards away was another defensive field, but it had been built by the Soviets.

An *MG-34* from the 4th company engaged in combat on the Donetz front (*Dernier Carré – Léon Degrelle*).

The enemy positions were in fact right in front, on the side of the hill. After about ten days of relative calm, the Burgundians received orders to prepare to attack. On the night between 16 and 17 May, the pioneer platoon of the *Oberfeldwebel* Mirgain and a platoon of heavy machine guns of the fourth company, infiltrated the barbed wire and minefields to take up a position in front of the enemy lines, taking advantage of the darkness. *Oberfeldwebel* Lassois, directed this group of about sixty Walloons, to which were added the German infantrymen of an infantry company. The offensive to drive back the Soviets beyond the Donetz was now imminent. At 02:30 in the morning, the codeword *'Donetz'* was transmitted to all units: it was the signal of the battle for hundreds of thousands of men who had to reduce the Soviet bridgehead in the Izjum region. ***(To be continued)***

Bibliography

M. Afiero, "*Belgian Waffen-SS Legion & Brigade 1941–44*", Osprey Publishing
M. Afiero, "*Rex Vaincra: Leon Degrelle e la Legione Wallonie*", Soldiershop Publishing
M. Afiero, "*Wallonie*", Marvia Edizioni
E. de Bruyne e M. Rikmenspoel, "*For Rex and for Belgium*", Helion & Company
L. Degrelle, "*Fronte dell'Est*", editrice Sentinella d'Italia
J. Mabire, "*Légion Wallonie au front de l'Est 1941-44*", Presses de la Cité

Danish volunteers on the Eastern front 1941-1943 - part 2

by Massimiliano Afiero

In the Demyansk pocket

The *Frikorps Danmark* was assigned to the northern sector of the Eastern Front, as a reinforcement troop for the SS *Totenkopf* division, which remained encircled in the Demyansk pocket, immediately after the Soviet winter counter-offensive. On May 7, 1942, the Danish volunteers were transferred to the Posen railway station and the next day, the entire unit landed at the military airport of Heiligensberg, about fifty kilometers south of Königsberg. Here, the Danes were loaded onto *Ju-52* transport aircraft, to be transferred to the Demyansk area. The first units to leave were the 2. and *3.Kompanie* and the 'heavy weapons' platoon of the *1.Kompanie*. Meanwhile, the rest of the *1.Kompanie* and the *4.Kompanie* were headquartered in some *Luftwaffe* depots and left the following day. The planes arrived as far as Pskov, a city that served as a border between the area of operations and the territory under civil administration, the *Ostland* Commissariat. In Pskov, the volunteers boarded other *Ju-52*s, this time armed for defense against possible enemy air attacks and this greatly disturbed the Danish volunteers themselves.

Danish volunteers at Heiligenberg military airport, waiting to board the *Ju-52* transport aircraft.

The new Ju-52s, escorted by German fighters, flew to Demyansk. *Freikorps* members were received at Demyansk airport by a convoy of *Totenkopf* trucks and later the divisional commander, *SS-Gruf.* Theodor Eicke himself came to greet the officers of the unit one by one. The military situation at that time appeared desperate and the arrival of a new reinforcement battalion was greeted positively by Eicke. Between 8 and 9 May, the units of the *Frikorps Danmark* took up positions in five villages off the Pola River: the *2.Kompanie* in Verezniza, the *1.Kp.* in Ignatizy and Karpovo, the *4.Kp.* in Podberesje, the General Staff and the *3.Kp.* in Zemena. All these villages were ten to fifteen kilometers apart from each other and were located southeast of the location of Vassiljevschtischina.

The situation of the German forces in the Demyansk pocket in May 1942.

Theodor Eicke, 1942.

The Danish companies were all located near the front line and their elements were immediately engaged mainly in building new defensive works, reinforcing existing ones and launching scouting patrols in advance in enemy territory. The impact of the Danish volunteers with the reality of the front was not the happiest: in the Demjansk pocket there were no *Panzers* or the *Stukas* of Göring. To the Danish soldiers, who only knew about the war from newsreels, the Blitzkrieg seemed a long way off. Here, as in much of the Eastern Front, the units of the German army were stuck in trench warfare reminiscent of the Great War. In particular, the Demyansk region itself was an area full of swamps and scrubs. The water was contaminated, the men lived in wet bunkers, where millions of mosquitoes spread a malaria-like disease, "*swamp fever*". The commander of the 1st Company, Per Sörensen, wrote to his parents that only a few hours of rain had turned the streets into a swamp and he walked in the mud up to his knees. The waterlogged ground was unable to absorb the rain, which made the bunkers and trenches virtually unusable: *"Unfortunately, it has been raining for two days and nights in a row now and most of the men escaped from the bunkers last night, around one o'clock, because they were afraid of drowning you. If this continues, we will have to live in the open. "*

Horse-drawn carts and motor vehicles move on a track between mud and water (*Lars Larsen*).

Danish volunteers engaged in marching in the swamps.

Officially the *Frikorps* was placed under the SS *Totenkopf* division, at that time divided into two fighting groups, the *Kampfgruppe Eicke* to the west of the pocket and the *Kampfgruppe Simon* to the east of the same. For the determined and valiant resistance of its soldiers during the previous Soviet winter counter-offensive, *SS-Gruf.* Eicke, had been decorated with Oak Leaves for his Knight's Cross. On May 12, 1942, *Frikorps* officers attended a war meeting, chaired by Eicke himself, in his Losnizy headquarters. The orders for the *Frikorps* members continued to be of static defense, so during this first period at the front, the Danish volunteers were not involved in any major combat, but only in some exploratory actions and in the reclamation of the land from Soviet mines. The Legion was located between the River Lovat and the position of Vassiljevschtischina: this area was baptized by the same volunteers as the *'tube'*. The Danish positions were anchored to the south, for about three kilometers, along the Robya

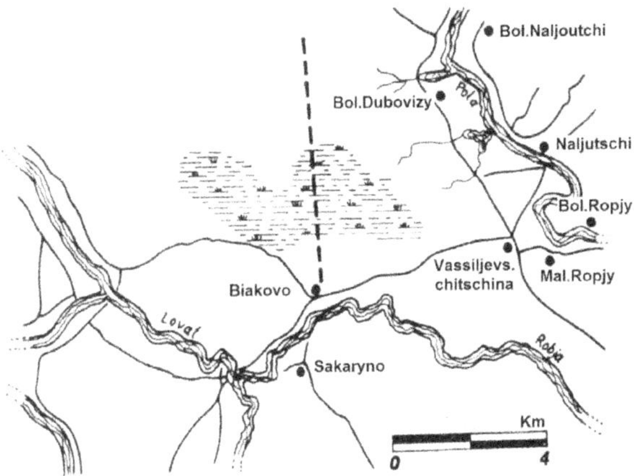

Area of employment of the Danish Legion on the Demyansk front, Spring 1942.

Motorcyclists of the staff of the *Frikorps Danmark*, in the Demyansk pocket, May 1942 (*Pierre Tiquet Collection*).

A *MG-34* on a defensive position, Spring 1942.

River: the river was dry and this favored enemy penetrations.

Early fighting

During the night, between 19 and 20 May, a formation of about two hundred Soviet soldiers managed to infiltrate the southern part of the *'tube'*, threatening the supply line. On the 20th, the *Frikorps* was placed on alert, after which transport vehicles arrived to transfer the volunteers to the area where the penetration had taken place. *SS-Stubaf.* Von Schalburg went to the command post of *SS-Tot.Inf.Rgt.2,* under the orders of *SS-Staf.* Helmuth Becker, in Biakovo, to have a more complete view of the situation. The *1.Kp./FD* was sent to the area southwest of Biakovo, while *2.Kp./FD* took position between the left flank of *1.Kp.*, towards the east, and the pioneer platoon, placed on the flank right of the same *1.Kp*. On May 21, the *3.* and *4. Kp.* also arrived in position, but both were placed in reserve in the area west of Biakovo. The light infantry guns and anti-tank pieces of *4.Kp.* were positioned behind the infantry companies.

At 18:00 on May 20, a strong Soviet company attacked the sector occupied by the *1.* and *2.Kp./FD*, supported by the fire of some heavy mortars. The Danish volunteers faced the assault with great courage, but when the situation began to get critical, a platoon of *3.Kp.* was sent to reinforce it.

Danish volunteers marching through the marshes.

Per Sörensen (second from the left) with *SS-Stubaf.* von Schalburg and other officers (*Lars Larsen*).

The Soviets were very surprised at the strong resistance put up by the Danes, thinking that they were facing a weak vanguard of the *Totenkopf.*

On the afternoon of May 21, a company of *Kampfgruppe Becker,* including elements of *SS-Tot.Inf.Rgt.2,* came to reinforce *2.Kp./FD. SS-Stubaf.* von Schalburg led this group, together with two platoons of *3.Kp.,* in a counterattack in the swampy forest south of Biakovo. A brief but bitter confrontation ensued, at the end of which the Soviets were forced to retreat. When the fighting stopped, more than eighty enemy soldiers lay on the ground and numerous prisoners were captured. Commander von Schalburg used his perfect knowledge of the Russian language to be able to gather information from these prisoners. By talking to them amicably, offering cigarettes and alcohol, he was able to obtain detailed information on the positions of the Soviet forces and their size. This valuable information proved crucial for the success of the operations conducted in the following days. Meanwhile, after a few hours of rest, *2.Kompanie* was moved back to the front line, this time to the west of the positions occupied by *1.Kp.* On May 22nd, *3.Kp.* of *SS-Hstuf.* Poul Neergaard-Jacobsen, was engaged in a roundup: at dawn, the company moved to a wider front, having to face a strong enemy group, stationed on a hill in the middle of the swamp. Led by their commander, the Danish volunteers launched an assault on the hill, but the strong barrage unleashed by the Soviets forced them to retreat soon after. A single platoon was then sent forward to attempt to outflank the enemy position and hit it from behind. Threatened to be surrounded, the Soviets retreated to another hill. A new attack by the Danes was again repelled. Determined to annihilate the enemy force, *SS-Hstuf.* Neergaard-Jacobsen gathered his men and threw them forward again: the enemy bullets filled the air, taking many victims. The company aide was shot dead and so was *SS-Ustuf.* Hans K.P. Nordholm.

SS-Hstuf. **Neergaard-Jacobsen.**

Once again, the attack was interrupted and the losses were counted: *3.Kompanie* complained of three dead and eight wounded. On the Soviet side, there were about twenty dead and wounded and 14 prisoners were captured. At 4:00 pm, new supplies of ammunition arrived, so the men of the third company returned to advance through the marshes around the hill defended by the enemy. Soviet artillery began firing at them, to cover the retreat of their soldiers towards the Robya River, where they settled along the southern bank. At that point, *SS-Hstuf.* Neergaard-Jacobsen decided to return to Biakovo.

The action of his company had prevented the Soviets from bringing aid to their troops deployed against the German rearguard and at the same time, the defensive line along the Robya River was stabilized. The Soviets responded by throwing massive fire from their artillery and multiple *'Katiuscia'* rocket launchers onto the Danish positions: it was the first time that Danish volunteers suffered the terrifying effect of *'Stalin's organs'*. When the bombing was over, the Soviets launched an infantry company to attack the positions of the *Frikorps*. Without losing heart and very calmly, the Danish volunteers set up their machine guns and opened fire.

A defensive position with a *MG-34* on the Demyansk front, Spring 1942 (NARA).

A Soviet platoon, however, managed to penetrate the right wing of the 1st Kompanie, so an assault troop was immediately gathered that managed to contain the penetration.

Soldiers of *Frikorps Danmark*, Spring 1942.

A defensive position on the Robya River, 1942.

At the end of the fighting, the first company had suffered six dead and eight wounded: among the fallen, a platoon commander, *SS-Oscha.* Alfred Thyssen Oksen and the commander of the pioneer platoon, *SS-Ustuf.* Niels Vive Falgaard. At the same time, many Soviet soldiers had abandoned their weapons and had voluntarily deserted in order to serve alongside the Germans: some of these deserters were selected to serve as auxiliaries (*Hilfswilliger*). Among the *'Hiwis'* who joined the Danes, there was also a young man of 14, named Pytor, who soon became the mascot of the *Frikorps.* Thereafter, he continued to serve in the *Danmark* Regiment until the final battle of Berlin.

Fights on the Robya River

Due to the size of the front sector assigned to *Frikorps,* it was decided to also transfer the reserve company to the front line as early as May 22, when *3. Kompanie* was deployed on the left wing (east). The infantry platoon behind *1.Kompanie,* changed position, to support *3.Kp.* This new deployment of forces brought the Danish volunteers one and a half kilometers west of Biakovo, with all units in the front line. From west to east, the German positions along the Robya were organized as follows: in Novoselje, two battalions of the *Totenkopf* with reduced ranks, with a bridgehead near the confluence of the Lovat River with the Robya; on the flank, facing the northern bank of the Robya was the *Frikorps* pioneer platoon; then followed *2.Kompanie* with a platoon of *3.Kp., 1.Kompanie* and *3.Kompanie,* the latter at the extreme left wing of the defensive line, which ended in Sakaryno, where the positions of the *126.Inf.Div.* began. The entire defensive line of the Danish Legion extended for about five kilometers, with the command placed behind the positions of *1. Kompanie.* The land occupied by the Danes was swampy and thick with vegetation, full of birch trees and weeds. The *Frikorps* soldiers were hard at work building underground bunkers and shelters, with great difficulty, given the lack of viable roads and tracks.

Soldiers of the *Frikorps Danmark* stop on the outskirts of a village before an operation, May 1942 (*Lars Larsen collection*).

A well camouflaged *bunker* in the forest (*Lars Larsen*).

Soldiers of the *Frikorps Danmark* in a trench, May 1942.

At the same time, the activity of the scouting patrols continued, which resulted in dozens of other enemy prisoners. On May 25, while the men of the 1st and 2nd Kompanie were working in the open air to reinforce their positions, they were suddenly targeted by Soviet heavy weapons fire: *SS-Ustuf.* Karl Wahle, platoon leader in the 1st Kompanie, was among the fallen. During the night between 26 and 27 May, a new reconnaisssance mission was carried out, after the Soviets had crossed the Robya River again, attempting to establish a bridgehead in the bend of the river north-west of the Danish positions, near of the village of Ssutoki. Bunkers had already been built and it was clear that the enemy intended to use this area as a launch base for new attacks. *SS-Stubaf.* von Schalburg, after receiving the information from his scouts, immediately gathered his company commanders: "*.... the Frikorps Danmark will attack the enemy beachhead with an assault troop during the next night and destroy it*". The mission was assigned to the second platoon of the 1st Kompanie, under the orders of *SS-Ustuf.* Just Nielsen(1). The latter, after having assembled his platoon, explained the mission: every soldier had to know exactly what he had to do.

***SS-Stubaf.* Christian von Schalburg among his men, before attacking Soviet positions, May 1942 (*Pierre Tiquet Collection*).**

***SS-Ustuf.* Just Nielsen.**

The direction of the attack was indicated on a map. All identification papers were left at the company's command post in case things didn't go well. Exactly at midnight on May 27, the order to march began: in total silence, the attack force began to move in complete darkness, covering more than seven hundred meters, without making the slightest noise. The men advanced in combat formation, paying attention to the presence of any enemy patrols. To avoid getting lost, each soldier was tied to the other with a piece of rope. Numerous hand grenades had been distributed, which the volunteers had placed in their boots and belts. At one point, the group split in half, to try to take the enemy by surprise. Shortly thereafter, they came near the Robya River, where the Soviets were in turmoil. A Soviet reconnaissance platoon was in fact taking up position on the bridgehead just at that moment. The Danes hid in the vegetation, holding their breath. The Soviets passed in front of them without perceiving anything, then set off for the bridgehead. The Danish volunteers in turn continued on to the Soviet wooden bunkers: *SS-Ustuf.* Nielsen was able to see an enemy guard post only at the last moment. After throwing a grenade into it, he ordered the assault: the loud detonation suddenly triggered hell in the calm of the night.

Soldiers of *Frikorps Danmark*, an *MG-34* squad, during an attack, May 1942.

A mortar of *Frikorps Danmark* in action, May 1942.

Weapons of all kinds opened fire, grenades exploded, machine guns crackled dully. The surprise was total and resistance was almost nil. The two Danish strike groups subjected the Soviet positions to a deadly crossfire. The Soviets fled in panic, through the woods or jumping into the river. Danish volunteers collected abandoned enemy weapons and placed explosives in enemy entrenchments to destroy them. The mission could be considered accomplished, therefore *SS-Ustuf.* Nielsen gave the order to go back. But just at that moment, a fiery hell broke out from the opposite bank of the river, pinning the Danish volunteers to the ground. Nielsen himself was shot while on the edge of the river, falling

Soldier of *Frikorps Danmark*, May 1942.

Transport of a wounded soldier after a combat, May 1942.

into its waters. Nobody managed to recover it and the Robya became his tomb. The group led by *SS-Oscha.* Kern found refuge among the devastated Soviet bunkers. Enemy fire forced them to stay under cover for a long time. In any case, to get to safety, the volunteers had to get out of the range of enemy fire, so one at a time, Kern's men began to retreat into a nearby wood, also taking five wounded with them, one of whom died shortly after in the field hospital, due to the serious injuries suffered. After regrouping in the woods, *SS-Oscha.* Kern assumed command of all the survivors and led them to the lines of the *Frikorps*. The seriously injured were placed on emergency beds, built with branches, while the lighter ones were helped by their comrades. *SS-Ustuf.* Nielsen was mentioned in the Hall of Honor of the German Army and the commander von Schalburg, at the news of his death, exclaimed: "*... I have lost one of my best officers*". Numerous Danish volunteers who had participated in the action were decorated with the Iron Cross.

In the following days, the activity of the reconnaissance patrols intensified considerably on both sides and numerous prisoners were captured. In retaliation, the Soviets resumed regularly hitting the *Frikorps* positions with their artillery, causing casualties, mostly wounded, to be recorded almost every day. Thanks to the activity of the patrols, an attempt by the Soviets to re-establish the newly destroyed bridgehead was detected. Under the direction of *SS-Ustuf.* Kure[(2)], commander of the infantry gun platoon, the heavy weapons of the Danish unit concentrated their fire on the

SS-Ustuf. Ole Peter Kure.

SS-Hstuf. Knud Børge Martinsen.

bridgehead causing considerable losses to the enemy. The Soviets, however, continued their work, operating mainly at night. This made it necessary to prepare a new operation against the enemy bridgehead, this time with the aim of definitively annihilating it and incorporating it into the Danish defensive lines, so as to definitively dispel any further future threat.

Von Schalburg put his second, *SS-Hstuf.* Knud Børge Martinsen, at the head of the new attack on the salient of Ssutoki. In support, there would be heavy weapons and artillery. The plan was that a platoon of *2.Kp./FD*, under the orders of *SS-Oscha.* Lasse Christensen attacked to the west, while another platoon of *1.Kp./FD*, under the orders of *SS-Oscha.* Stadtscheid, attacked from the east. Both platoons were then to join up along the river. Two cover groups, each with two machine guns, under the orders of *SS-Oscha.* Leo Madsen and *SS-Uscha.* Jens Nielsen, were to occupy strategic positions to support the two assault platoons. At 02:00 on June 2, the cover platoons emerged from the woods and moved to their assigned positions. At 02.45 am, the assault platoons arrived at their starting positions. At the crack of dawn, the *Frikorps'* heavy weapons opened fire on the Soviet bridgehead for about three minutes. Then they changed positions in order to hit the Soviet artillery positions on the other side of the river. This cover of fire allowed a reserve group to take up positions behind the main attack group. Once the concentrated fire of the heavy weapons ceased, the Danish volunteers launched into the attack.

The death of the commander

The first phase of the operation seemed to end with complete success. The two assault platoons managed to penetrate the most advanced enemy positions, but soon after, they were blocked by Soviet artillery and mortar fire. The most advanced platoon still managed to make it to the beachhead, but the accurate Soviet fire effectively countered the action of cover groups, wounding both platoon leaders. *SS-Stubaf.* von Schalburg, who was with the reserve force, realized the gravity of the situation, so he went to the front line to support his soldiers.

Advancing in front of his men, von Schalburg landed on an enemy mine, being seriously wounded in the leg. When his soldiers approached him to try to help him, he pushed them away with his hand, shouting: "... *Go ahead guys, keep attacking!*". Just then, some Soviet mortar rounds swooped around him. Von Schalburg's orderly, *Sturmmann* Jonstrup and two other Danish soldiers still decided to help their commander. But when they got close, another mortar round hit them in full. *SS-Stubaf.* von Schalburg and two Danish volunteers died instantly.

The last photo of *SS-Stubaf.* Von Schalburg before he was killed on 2 June 1942 (*Lars Larsen*).

***Sturmmann* Alfred Jonstrup.**

Sturmmann Jonstrup threw himself into the shelter of a tree while still being wounded. Jonnstrup himself and some pioneers shortly afterwards managed to take away the bodies of the commander and the other two fallen volunteers.

SS-Hstuf. Martinsen, busy directing the fire of heavy weapons, when he received the news of the death of the commander, ordered the suspension of the attack, now in a phase of stalemate.

However, the withdrawal of the Danish volunteers turned into a disaster, as the Soviets continued to target them with their deadly fire. When the survivors reached their positions, the losses were counted: 28 fallen and numerous wounded, three of whom died shortly after at the rescue post.

SS-Stubaf. **Christian Frederik von Schalburg.**

Soldiers pause to pay their respects at the cemetery.

Report of SS-Hstuf. Martinsen on the progress of the attack: "... *On June 2, 1942, at 01:00, we prepared to launch an assault forward to prepare the front line. To accomplish this mission, von Schalburg decided to engage two assault platoons, protected from the fire of all our heavy weapons. A careful exploratory action was carried out, as well as all the necessary precautions were taken and every detail was taken care of, to dispel any problem .... All the preparations for the operation were carefully hidden from the sight of the enemy and were mainly done at night and with the utmost precaution. The troop participated with total self-denial and interest ... The night passed quietly. On the part of the enemy, no movement was observed ... At 01:00, the units began to move ... Our commander had followed the assault staying on the left wing. Unfortunately, the terrain had not been explored at that point ... Surely von Schalburg had the impression that the attack was not taking place as quickly as possible, so he went forward, insulting the Soviets in their language, which he had known since his childhood in Imperial Russia. During this advance, he was wounded by the explosion of a mine and at the same time, a mortar shell ended his life.* "

That was a tragic day for the *Frikorps Danmark*: the men of the anti-tank unit were busy digging graves for the fallen, along the main road, near Biakovo. The next day, a small convoy of horses, towing wagons of peasants, transported the bodies of the Danish dead

A simple grave for the commander of *Frikorps Danmark*.

Danish volunteers on a defensive position, 1942.

from the battalion command post to the place of burial. On the first cart was the body of von Schalburg, wrapped in the *'Dannebrog'*, the Danish national flag. *SS-Staf.* Helmuth Becker, of the SS *Totenkopf* division, came to attend the ceremony, during which von Schalburg's post-mortem promotion to the rank of *SS-Obersturmbannführer* was announced, on specific orders from *Reichsführer-SS* Heinrich Himmler. Also, the commander of the *Wiking*, Felix Steiner, who had had von Schalburg under his orders, drew up a special agenda, on 9 June 1942, to commemorate the death of the valiant Danish officer. On June 18, 1942, the official funeral ceremony for the commander of *Frikorps Danmark* was held in Copenhagen, an official act of the Danish state, attended by various ministers and important military and civilian personalities on behalf of the government. On the Eastern Front, *SS-Hstuf.* Knud Børg Martinsen took over the command of the Legion on a temporary basis.

The attack on Bolschoje-Dubovizy

Despite the failure recorded in the Robya River sector, the Danish Legion began to be regarded by the German commands as a reliable combat formation, as a result of which they were assigned more demanding missions. Northeast of the *Frikorps* positions, near Biakovo, the Soviets had established a new bridgehead on the Pola River, threatening the German defensive front in that sector. *SS-Staf.* Becker, in command of *SS-Tot.Inf.Rgt.1*, was in charge of defense in that same area. To block the Soviets, Becker drew up a plan that was to engage the *I. Bataillon* of his regiment, the Motorcycle Battalion (*Kradsch.Btl.*) of *SS-Stubaf.* Franz Kleffner and the *Frikorps Danmark*. The *I./Tot.Inf.Rgt.1*, under the orders of *SS-Hstuf.* Emil Zollhöfer and the *Frikorps*, had to attack the Soviet positions at Bolschoje-Dubovizy from the west, passing through four kilometers of marshes, while Kleffner's motorcyclists had to proceed along the main road, moving from the south. To participate in this new mission, the Danish volunteers had to modify their deployment: during the night between 3 and 4 June, they left their old positions and passed through the lines of *126.Infanterie-Division*, heading towards the area of the forest north of Biakovo, where preparations for the attack were in full swing. For most of the day, Danish volunteers were busy cleaning their weapons and preparing ammunition. At around 18:00, *SS-Hstuf.* Martinsen, received orders for the deployment of his units, then inspected the troops and spoke to several of his soldiers. Morale was high, the men were eager to avenge the death of their commander. At dawn, the units began to move: two companies of *8.leichte Infanterie-Division* led the assault column, immediately followed by the Danish volunteers, in turn followed by *I./Tot.Inf.Rgt.1*. The heavy weapons of the *Frikorps* were attached to the Kleffner Motorcycle Battalion. The main column of the *Frikorps* marched on a path through the swamp, a little more than a meter wide and partly covered with water. From time to time, the mules carrying the ammunition got bogged down, slowing the march. It took seven hours to cross the swamp.

***SS-Staf.* Hellmuth Becker.**

Men of *Frikorps Danmark* study a map, June 1942.

A group of *Frikorps Danmark* soldiers in the forest.

Danish volunteers aboard a truck before an operation.

SS soldiers in the Bolschoje-Dubovizy area, June 1942.

At about 3:00 am on June 5, the units arrived at the starting positions for the attack: the two army companies occupied cover positions to the north and west. Just south of them were the Danish volunteers, who represented the northern wing of the attack front, while on the right flank, was the *Totenkopf* battalion, which was to lead the attack on the southern wing. The movement of the German units did not go unnoticed by the Soviets, as demonstrated by the mortar fire that began to fall on the heads of the attackers.

At 4:00 the attack began: the *Frikorps* advanced with *2.Kompanie,* under the orders of *SS-Ostuf.* Hansen, on the left wing and the 1st Kompanie, under the orders of *SS-Ostuf.* Per Sörensen, on the right wing. The *3.Kompanie* of *SS-Hstuf.* Neergaard-Jacobsen remained in reserve, but still close to the attacking elements. The Danish volunteers approached the Soviet positions, under the cover of a forest southwest of Bol.Dubovizy, immediately encountering strong resistance. Among the bunkers in front of them was a Soviet reserve battalion, determined to resist to the bitter end. This forced the men of the *Frikorps* to fall back towards the woods, to avoid suffering serious losses. The German artillery supported the action, but failed to completely dampen the resistance of the Soviets. At around 8:00, *SS-Hstuf.* Martinsen, sent *3.Kp./FD* forward as reinforcement on the right wing, in order to renew the attack. But once again a massive Soviet barrage prevented any forward progress: *SS-Hstuf.* Neergaard-Jacobsen was injured and his replacement, *SS-Ostuf.* Henneke(4), followed the same fate a few minutes later. *SS-Ustuf.* Alfred Nielsen then assumed command of the company.

***SS-Ostuf.* Heinz Henneke.**

By 10:00, most of the *Frikorps* elements had arrived about 500 meters west of Bol.Dubovizy. On the right of the Danes, *I./Tot.Inf.Rgt.1* had kept the same pace, while *SS-Stubaf.* Kleffner continued to lead his motorcyclists south, covered in a curtain of fire created by assault guns, infantry guns, and anti-tank guns. Three assault guns, supported by SS infantrymen, advancing in front of the other units, managed to overwhelm the Soviet positions. The enemy laid down their weapons and surrendered. Thanks to the rapid advance of Kleffner's men, the *Frikorps* managed to cross the bunker line in front of it. But even after this leap forward, the attack halted again, this time to give the men time to catch their breath, receive supplies and evacuate the numerous wounded. The Soviets brought their artillery into action, striking their newly lost positions. Kleffner's units were forced to change positions several times, to avoid the deadly fire of the Soviet artillery, which followed them with deadly precision. Somewhere, there must have been an artillery observer directing the enemy fire: after several searches, he was finally found in a hole dug in the ground.

***SS-Stubaf.* Franz Kleffner.**

Second phase of the attack

At 10:30, the second phase of the attack began, initially focusing a massive heavy weapon fire on Bol.Dubovizy's position. Soon after, Kleffner's cyclists and *3./Tot.Inf.Rgt.1* made their way to the southern part of the village. The attack of the *Frikorps* against the enemy positions to the north and west, however, was still blocked. The Soviets continued to defend the northern part of Bol Dubovizy with extreme determination, inflicting heavy losses on the Danish units. The wounded were transported across the swamp, drawn in makeshift horse-drawn carts, to the battalion's rescue post in Biakovo, where the *Frikorps* health workers were under the orders of *SS-Ostuf.* Dr. Lotze. German artillery hit the northern part of Bol Dubovizy again and shortly thereafter it appeared that the Soviet defenses began to fail. At 2.15pm, Danish volunteers finally broke into the village, supported by three assault guns from *Kampfgruppe Kleffner*.

SS-Ostuf. **Sörensen with his men, before the attack.**

A Danish volunteer makes a gruesome discovery.

The soldiers moved from house to house, engaging in fierce hand-to-hand clashes with the Soviets and only after about an hour, the resistance ceased as the remaining Soviet soldiers retreated north. The *Frikorps* men along with the *Totenkopf* infantry battalion continued to advance, establishing a new defensive line north of the village. Two hours later, a Soviet counterattack, supported by three tanks, invested these positions: the Danes expected it and were ready. Some enemy groups managed to overcome the first positions and reach the first houses of the village, but were soon after, rejected by the SS volunteers, thanks also to the fire support of the heavy weapons. At sunset, the new defensive positions were hit by Soviet artillery fire and the bombardment lasted all night.

From the operational log of the *1.Kp./FD*, dated June 6, 1942: "*.... During the night, there was a great air activity. Many bombers attacked the position of Bol.Dubovizy at 2:50 and soon after, Artillery bombardment also intervened. At 4:00, the enemy attacked with five tanks. Our assault guns counterattacked and destroyed two enemy tanks. At 5:10, the attack stopped. At 9:00, we another enemy attack occurred, first with artillery and then with tanks and infantry. But it was again repulsed. During the rest of the day no enemy movement was observed in the company sector.* ". Soviet losses had been high. For the first time, the Danish volunteers were confronted with the *'suicide'* attacks by the Soviets, under the impulse of the Communist political commissars, real killer beasts. A captured Soviet officer testified:

A soldier of *Frikorps Danmark* with a destroyed Russian T34-76 tank (*Lars Larsen Collection*).

"... *We have enough men. We are only short of tanks and ammunition.*" The significance of this statement was clear: human resources could be sacrificed to make up for the lack of adequate armament. Later, thanks to 'generous' loans from the United States, the Communists had fewer problems ... Putting into practice the old *Waffen SS* maxim that "... *sweat saves blood*", the Danish volunteers were busy building new defensive positions in the short periods of respite. During the night between 5 and 6 June, they had in the meantime been reinforced by a company of *290. Inf.Div.* A few days of relative calm followed, during which *SS-Hstuf.* Martinsen took advantage of this to deliver more Iron Crosses to his men.

Notes

(1) Johannes Just Nielsen, born on 6 July 1920 in Darum. He initially served in *2.Kompanie* of the *Frikorps* before moving on to the *1.Kp.*

(2) Ole Peter Kure, born on 29 October 1917 in Vestermarie / Bornholm. He had previously served in *4./Nordland* (January 1942), before being transferred to *4./FD.*

(3) Boy Harald Hansen, born May 13, 1920 in Flensburg, SS-Nr. 372 384. Previously he had served as *Sturmmann* in *3./LSSAH* (1939).

(4) Heinz Henneke, born January 14, 1912 in Staßfurt in Germany, SS-Nr. 312 936.

Bibliography

Massimiliano Afiero,"*Frikorps Danmark: i volontari danesi sul fronte dell'Est, 1941-1943*", Associazione Culturale Ritterkreuz

Jens Pank Bjerregaard, Lars Larsen, "*Danish Volunteers of the Waffen-SS: Freikorps Danmark 1941-43*", Helion & Co Ltd

Richard Landwehr, "*La Estirpe de Thor: el cuerpo franco SS Danés en la campana de Rusia, 1941-43*", Garcia Hispan Editor

The SS-Division 'Nord' and Operation Barbarossa

by Massimiliano Afiero

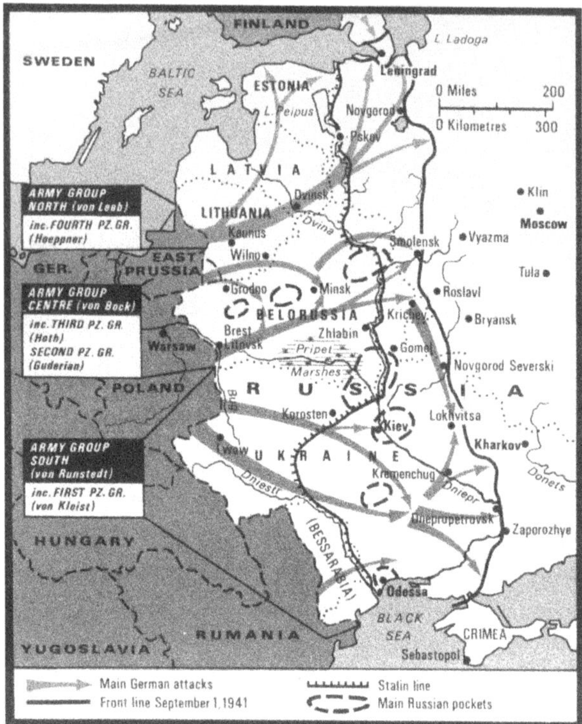

At dawn on Sunday, June 22, 1941, the armies of the Third Reich attacked the Soviet Union: along a front that ran from the Baltic Sea to the Black Sea, millions of German soldiers invaded Soviet territory overrunning everything and everyone. The greatest military invasion in history had begun. The news spread throughout the world, and all of Germany's allies acted quickly to declare war on the USSR, to take part in the battle against Bolshevism. German propaganda devoted itself to transforming the invasion into a veritable crusade which pitted European civilization against the Soviet communist barbarians. The German invasion plan called for attacking in three directions: to the north, the Army Group under Marshal von Leeb, with twenty-nine divisions of which three were armored, was to move from East Prussia, pass through the Baltic countries and then aim towards Leningrad. In addition an offensive thrust was planned to seize the important commercial port Murmansk, in the extreme north of Finnish Lapland. In the center, von Bock's Army Group numbering fifty divisions, of which nine were armored, jumping off from Poland was to skirt the Pripet Marshes from the north and head first to Minsk and then to Moscow. To the south, the Army Group under von Rundstedt with forty divisions, of which five were armored, was to invade the Ukraine and the Donets Basin, and then the Caucasus with its rich oil deposits. The ultimate objective was the conquest of all of European Russia from Archangel on the White Sea to

A German motorized column in Russia, June 1941.

Hitler conferring with General Dietl, on the left.

Finnish infantry marching towards the front, June 1941.

A German motorized column in Finnish Lapland, 1941.

Astrakhan on the Caspian Sea. The two wings of the German attack front were constituted by satellite forces: in the far north of Finland, in Karelia, there were sixteen Finnish divisions under Marshal Mannerheim, reinforced by five German divisions. On the far south of the front were Romanian forces. Some time later these would be joined by Hungarian, Slovak, Croat and Italian forces. All of Europe had legitimate reasons to participate in the fight against Stalin. The Finns wanted to regain the territory they had lost to Soviet aggression in 1940.

The Finnish vendetta

After having suffered from the Soviet aggression of 1939, the Finns nurtured a vendetta against the Moscow government. In August 1940, the Finnish government had begun secret negotiations with Germany for military cooperation: the Germans furnished arms and equipment to the Finns in exchange for permission for German troops to transit their territory to reach northern Norway. The Germans considered Finnish territory to be of great strategic value in an anti-Soviet context. In December 1940, a new agreement was signed that authorized the stationing of German troops in Finland, principally near the northern border with the Soviet Union. The German units were warmly welcomed by the

Finnish population. On the eve of the beginning of Operation *Barbarossa,* the Finnish troops in the northern part of the country were subordinated directly to the German headquarters. General mobilization was proclaimed on June 17. However, the Germans

Finnish soldiers crossing the 1940-agreed border (Moscow Peace Treaty) at the start of the 1941 invasion during the Continuation War against the Soviet Union.

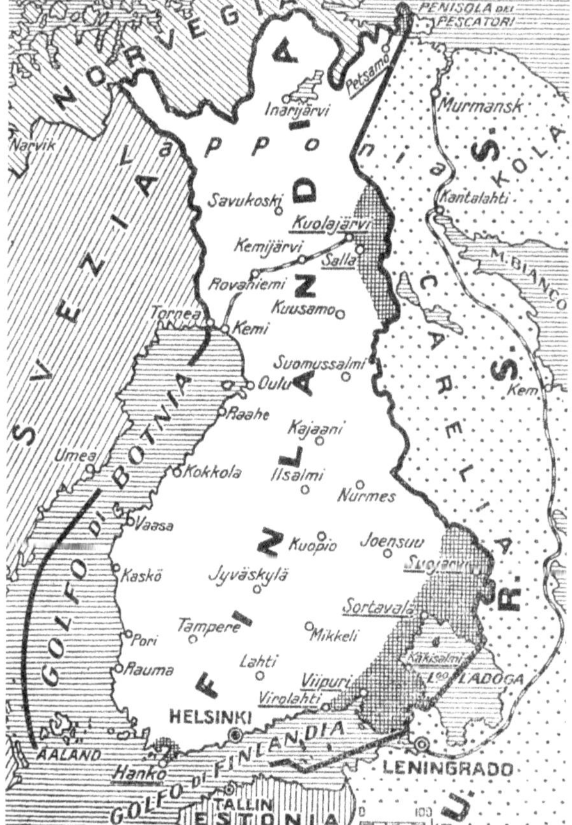

Map of the Finnish front. The hash-marked area was ceded by Finland to the USSR in 1940.

did not inform the Finns of the imminence of the attack until 21 June. The Finns decided not to initiate hostilities against the USSR immediately alongside the Germans, in order to avoid being seen as aggressors in the eyes of worldwide public opinion. It was only after Soviet aircraft had bombed the cities of Helsinki, Turku and Porvoo that Finland, as a nation that had been attacked, officially declared war on the Soviet Union on June 26, 1941.

Operation "Silberfuchs"

While planning Operation *Barbarossa,* the German strategists were well aware of the need to conquer the city of Murmansk with its important port; the port of Murmansk was in fact the only Russian port that was not closed by ice during the winter and thus was the only way possible for the Soviets to reach all of the seas of the world and at the same time to receive goods and carry out commercial exchanges. During the First World War, the Czar had a railway line built to link St.Petersburg with Murmansk, using German and Austrian

Dietl and von Falkenhorst discussing battle plans.

Dietl in typical Arctic tundra terrain.

General von Falkenhost with Finnish General Siilasvuo.

prisoners of war as the main source of labor. Hitler himself, in his talks with Eduard Dietl, commander of the *"Norwegen"* Mountain Corps, indicated Murmansk to be a primary military objective; by using the Leningrad-Murmansk railway line, Stalin could move large numbers of troops and equipment to the Finnish border, thereby threatening the Petsamo nickel mines and the Narvik mineral deposits, which were of vital interest to the German war economy. In addition, aerial reconnaissance had identified the existence in Murmansk of immense railway yards and industrial facilities, making the city a modern fortress on the Arctic Ocean which was only a hundred kilometers distant from the Petsamo mines. Considering thus the particular nature of the terrain, which would be difficult for a direct attack by motorized troops, Dietl and the other German generals were able to convince Hitler that to neutralize the base at Murmansk it would be enough to cut the Murmansk-Leningrad railway line. In elaborating the plan of attack, Operation *Rentier* (Reindeer) was "dusted off", which was an offensive action planned by the German general staff shortly after the Winter War between the Soviet Union and Finland; in the event that the two countries were to go to war again, two German mountain divisions were to have crossed the border between Norway and Finland and occupy the Petsamo region, in particular its nickel mines, to prevent it being occupied by the Soviets. Beginning with that operation, the staff of General Nikolaus

The original plan for operation Silver Fox.

German soldiers with a Soviet prisoner in the Murmansk area, Summer 1941.

von Falkenhorst, commander of the German occupation forces in Norway, planned operation *Silberfuchs* (Silver Fox): while the German mountain troops occupied Petsamo, another two divisions were to move from Salla and cut the railway line that linked Murmansk and Leningrad, conquering the city of Kandalaksha, and then move towards the port in a pincer movement. However, when the Finns decided to join in on the attack, von Falkenhorst was forced to revisit his plan and thus Operation *Silberfuchs* was divided into two phases which were to run contemporaneously: the *Gebirgs-Korps Norwegen*, under General Dietl, consisting of 2. and 3. *Gebirgs-Division*, a panzer company, two engineer battalions, elements of an anti-aircraft artillery group and a smoke-laying unit were to execute Operation *Platinfuchs* (Platinum Fox), a frontal attack on Murmansk starting from Petsamo, while the German XXXVI Corps under General Hans Feige consisting of *169.Inf.Div., SS-Division 'Nord'*, two tank battalions, two motorized artillery groups, two engineer battalions and elements of an anti-aircraft artillery group were instead to execute Operation *Polarfuchs* (Polar Fox), an attack against Kandalaksha to isolate Murmansk from the south. The Finnish III Army Corps under General Hjalmar Siilasvuo, consisting of the 3rd and 6th infantry divisions was to support *Polarfuchs* with an attack on the right of the XXXVI Corps. Other Finnish units were to support Dietl's attack, while most of the Finnish Army was to be committed further south, on the Karelian front. The *Luftwaffe* was to provide air support employing about sixty *Ju 87 Stuka* dive bombers, twenty fighters of various types, twenty bombers and about a dozen reconnaissance aircraft, divided equally between the two attack wings.

Difficult movement of *Nord* units towards the front.

General Dietl tried to oppose the decision to conduct both operations at the same time, thus dividing the few forces available. In addition he said that he was very concerned about the poor logistics situation, especially with respect to the arrival of reinforcements, which were to disembark first at Narvik and then be transferred overland, traveling over impossible roads in the Arctic tundra towards the front lines.

The attack against Salla

The *SS-Divison 'Nord'* had been integrated into General Feige's *XXXVI.Armee-Korps* that was deployed in front of Salla. On June 18, 1941 the SS units began began to march towards the Russo-Finnish border to prepare for the attack. The SS units had to cross ground that was both wooded and swampy, and which lacked roads or trails. Motor vehicles sank in the muck, and it was necessary to build corduroy roads with tree trunks to enable them to move. All the while, the soldiers had to march with protective nets over their heads to protect them from the bites of insects that infested the area. The assembly areas were reached with the utmost exertion and considerably later than had been planned. The main objective assigned to Feige's corps was to capture the Kandalaksha position, but first it was necessary for the Nord units to eliminate the Soviet positions in the area of Salla. The city had been annexed into the Soviet Union; in this sector, following the 1939/1940 war against the Finns, the Soviets had constructed solid defensive positions, especially minefields and anti-tank ditches, transferring many units there and deploying a good

SS motorcyclists stuck in the mud.

A *Nord* anti-tank unit moving towards the front.

number of artillery units. All of these preparations and the entire defensive system had escaped the notice of German reconnaissance, which had classified the areas as lightly defended, added to the fact that the size of the Soviet forces in the area was almost unknown. A few days before the start of the operations *SS-Brigdf.* Demelhuber deployed his units along quite a wide front with the objective of reaching the hills across the border that flanked the Kelloselka-Salla road. The attack by the ground units was to be preceded by an intense preparatory fire by German and Finnish artillery batteries.

Movement of German units

The movements of German units towards the assembly areas were spotted by Soviet reconnaissance and on June 26, enemy aircraft hit the positions of *SS-Inf.Rgt.7.* German aviation replied with a heavy bombardment of the Soviet positions. Reconnaissance patrols were sent out shortly thereafter to try to determine the strength of the enemy units and to nip in the bud any attempts to break through the German positions. The *Nord* then prepared to launch its frontal attack on both sides of the Rovaniemi-Alakurtti road. For the attack, it was reinforced by *Panzer-Abteilung z.b.V.40*, equipped with old *PzKpfw I* and a few PzKpfw II tanks. For the attack on Salla, this tank battalion was in turn reinforced by *6.Kp./SS-Inf.Rgt.6*, by a mortar platoon and an engineer platoon, all of which formed *Panzergruppe Tölke*, commanded by *Hauptmann* Tölke, commander of *2.Kp./Pz.Abt.40*. As previously stated, the mission assigned to the Nord units seemed simple enough, at least on paper: conquer the heights on both sides of the Kelloselka-Salla road about a kilometer east of the border and then continue on as far as the Keskimäinen-Särkivaara-Iso-Pieni line. This sector was defended by the Soviet 122nd Rifle Division, reinforced by several artillery and anti-aircraft batteries, as well as by a border guard regiment. To the left of *Nord* were units of *169.Inf.Div.*, and to the right were units of the Finnish 6th Infantry Division. The attack by *Nord* was to be carried out by *SS-Inf.Rgt.7*, supported by *I./SS-Inf.Rgt.6* on its southern flank. The remainder of *SS-Inf.Rgt.6* was to cover the north and south of Lake Onkanojärvi.

A *Nord* detachment passing by a machine gun squad that is resting.

***Nord* personnel on the eve of the offensive.**

Artillery support was to be provided by the batteries of *I./SS-Art.Rgt. "Nord"* and by batteries from *Korps-Art.Abt. 496* and *520*. In addition, the *Luftwaffe* was to provide several squadrons of *Stuka* dive-bombers which were to hit the Soviet artillery positions from the air before the ground attack began. On June 30, 1941, however, the Soviets made the first move, carrying out a spoiling attack along the Kelloselka-Salla road. The Soviets first used their artillery, then sent several infantry units forward; when German artillery in turn opened fire against the area covered by the attack, the Soviet units quickly fell back, mainly to avoid an encounter against German and Finnish units.

***Nord* personnel on the eve of the offensive on the Salla front, late June 1941.**

***Nord* troops attacking on the Salla front.**

The attack begins

The attack by *XXXVI.Armee-Korps* began at 14:00 on July 1, 1941, after intense preparatory artillery fire and support from above by the Stukas; the SS companies moved from their positions at 16:25. However, the preparatory fire had a collateral effect: in addition to hitting the enemy positions, it set the woods around Salla on fire, thus hindering the view of the artillery observers as well as of the supporting German aircraft. *I./SS-Inf.Rgt.7*, commanded by *SS-Stubaf.* Augsberger, was able to advance successfully for a few hundred meters, under cover of the woods and the smoke, but when the SS troops emerged from the forest they found themselves under a massive wall of fire from many Soviet machine guns; it was a veritable trap set up by the Soviet engineers who in that area had cut down all of the trees to allow better fields of fire. In addition, they had sown all of the nearby ground with mines and had prepared traps with wire obstacles. The entire advance element led by *SS-Ustuf.* Hering, an officer of *2./SS-Inf.Rgt.7,* sustained heavy casualties under the enemy fire. Following the initial setback, the heavy weapons entered into action and thanks to their covering fire the units were able to resume their advance and establish themselves in sheltered positions.

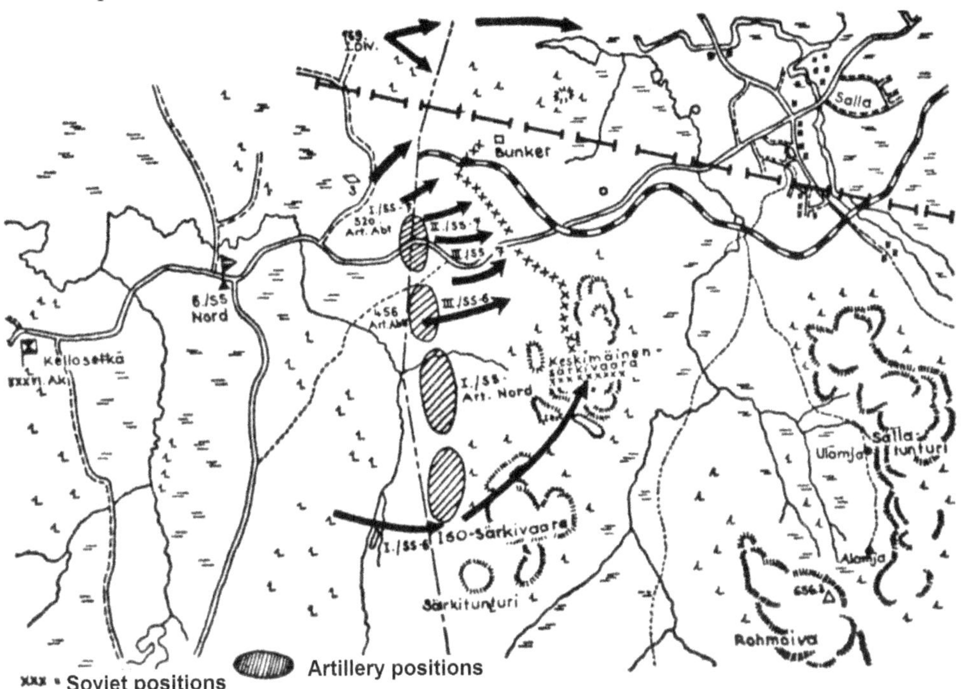

Axes of attack of SS troops on the Salla front, July 1941.

***Nord* artillery piece engaged in firing.**

The attack continued until *SS-Ustuf.* Hering himself was killed; left without a leader the men began to disperse in a precipitous manner. Taking advantage of the breakup of the SS units, the Soviets launched a counterattack, pursuing the fleeing Germans. Only a very few SS soldiers remained to defend their positions to the last round and were killed or captured by the Soviets. In an attempt to restore order to the German units, several companies of *II./SS-Inf.Rgt.7* were sent along the Rovaniemi-Salla road, but they were likewise stopped by the Soviet counterattack which was supported by several tanks.

A *Nord* soldier during an attack, July 1941.

Nord soldiers, during an attack, armed with a machine gun and hand grenades, July 1941.

Two *Nord* soldiers during the attack on Salla.

Hidden amongst the trees and bushes, Soviet and German soldiers fought fiercely in a series of close-quarter encounters, with no holds barred. Fearing for the fate of his soldiers, *SS-Ostubaf.* Willy Schinke, commander of *II./SS-Inf.Rgt.7*, gathered all of the men available to go to the aid of his two lead companies. In leading the attack, the officer was killed in front of the enemy positions. Once again, the loss of their leader caused the units to break up. The Soviets thus managed to throw the SS units back to where they had started from. In an attempt to regain control of the situation, *III./SS-Inf.Rgt.7* commanded by *SS-Stubaf.* Braun, which until then had been held in reserve, was brought into action and was thrown into the attack south of the Rovaniemi-Salla road, but even the offensive thrust by Braun's units was stopped by the strong resistance offered by the Soviets. Among the battalion dead was *SS-Hstuf.* Kurt Grabow, commander of *7./SS-Inf.Rgt.7*. I./*SS-Inf.Rgt.6* under *SS-Stubaf.* Schreiber, deployed on the southern flank of the attack front, after having managed to reach the foot of the Keskimäinen-Särkivaara heights, was stopped in front of a solid line of fortifications. On the left flank, the other SS units and *Panzergruppe Tölke* were bogged down in a swamp and at the end of the day were forced to go on the defensive in order to face a counterattack by enemy tanks. The rest of the day closed disastrously; along the entire front the SS *'Nord'* units had been thrown back and in several points the Soviets had counterattacked forcing the Germans to establish defensive positions further to the rear, leaving the task of stemming the enemy counteroffensive to other German units of *XXXVI.Armee-Korps.* The SS units had shown proof of their inexperience and lack of organization: little communication and coordination between units, attacks carried out in a disorganized fashion, heavy losses for little gain on the ground. In addition, many companies had given in to panic during the counterattacks mounted by the enemy.

***Nord* soldiers resuming the attack against Soviet positions, July 1941.**

A *Nord* soldier on the Salla front armed with a *Mauser* rifle.

The following day the division tried to resume the offensive; *I/SS-Inf.Rgt.6* and *II./SS-Inf.Rgt.7* were grouped together and formed *Kampfgruppe Schreiber*, with orders to maintain their positions along the Keskimäinen-Särkivaara line. But the day passed by sealing a breach between the positions of *III./SS-Inf.Rgt.7* and *II./SS-Inf.Rgt.7.* At the same time, the positions of *Kampfgruppe Schreiber* also were pulled further to the rear to ensure a more continuous front line. By around noon the new front line ran from Pekeloja and continued as far as

An NCO observing enemy positions, July 1941.

Wounded soldiers making their way to the rear.

Särkivaara. *II./SS-Inf.Rgt.6* commanded by *SS-Hstuf.* Elsner replaced *II./SS-Inf.Rgt.7,* which was placed in reserve.

On July 4, it was the Soviets who attacked; their tanks were able to open a gap in the German lines. Some elements of the divisional logistics train were gripped by panic and tried to flee towards Army Corps headquarters. *SS-Brigdf.* Demelhuber and several other SS officers managed to reestablish calm and to assemble the units once again. On the same day, a new attack against the enemy positions was attempted, but the Soviets were able to put up a solid resistance and inflict further losses on the Germans. Among those killed were two officers, *SS-Ustuf.* Walter Schwerer and *SS-Ustuf.* Walter Steinwerder, both from *7./SS-Inf.Rgt.7*. The next day, units of *169.Inf.Div.* were able to reach the Savukoski-Salla road which eased the pressure on the SS units a bit, enabling them to resume the attack despite the fact that the troops were demoralized following the humiliating defeats they had suffered during the previous days. The heights of Keskimäinen and Särkivaara were the objectives of the SS troops for that day. The divisional assault group was formed by *I./SS-Inf.Rgt.6, II./SS-Inf.Rgt.7* and *Pi.-Kp./SS-Inf.Rgt.6*. Because of the difficult terrain characterized by dense forests and swamps, it was not possible to bring up the heavy weapons to support the assault. The SS units once again found themselves in difficulty, having to attack without adequate supporting fire, and again suffering casualties without achieving any result. Likewise, the attack launched by *Gruppe Benner,* consisting of *II./6* (minus *5.Kp.*), a tank platoon, two engineer platoons, a platoon of light infantry support guns and an anti-tank platoon commanded by *SS-Hstuf.* Benner , met the same fate. *Verteidigungsgruppe Jens* (the "Jens" Defense Group), which was defending the front line, was subjected to a terrible bombardment by Soviet artillery for the entire afternoon.

Nord **machine gun crew with a Czech machine gun, July 1941.**

A *Nord* sniper in an *MG 34* defensive position.

The commander of *SS-Inf.Rgt.7, SS-Ostubaf.* Jens, was killed and many of his officers were wounded as a result of an artillery shell that hit and exploded in the regimental command post. On July 6, *I./SS-Inf.Rgt.6* again went on the attack, managing to reach the Keskimäinen-Sarkivaara line, but sustained heavy losses; among these was the commander of *3.Kp./SS-Inf.Rgt.6, SS-Ostuf.* Arnold Herold and *SS-Ustuf.* Karl Rösner, commander of *1.Kp./SS-Inf.Rgt.6*. Further to the north, units of *169.Infanterie-Division*. also were pushed back from in front of the Soviet positions at Salla. During the course of the following night the Soviet forces, threatened with encirclement by the Finnish 6th Division, ended up abandoning their positions.

SS soldiers carrying a wounded comrade.

Nord soldiers in a destroyed Soviet position (*P. Tiquet*).

On July 8, 1941, at 13:30, the city of Salla finally fell into the hands of the Finnish and German troops.

A heavy balance of losses

The battle for the conquest of Salla had cost the German forces very dearly, and particularly to units of *Nord*. The SS division's unhappy baptism of fire was the result of poor training of its men, as highlighted in Demelhuber's report, but also because of a lack of artillery and air support for the offensive action. In addition, the strength of the Soviet forces had been greatly underestimated by the German high command which, in order not to alert the enemy prior to the offensive, had not sent out reconnaissance patrols across the border to gather intelligence information. The losses sustained by Nord amounted to 261 men killed and missing and 307 wounded. On July 9, the SS division received orders to protect the southern flank of *XXXVI.Armee-Korps*. The reconnaissance group and *I./SS-Inf.Rgt.7* advanced as far as Lampela, occupying defensive positions that had been built by the Soviets. On July 11, *SS-Staf.* Ballauf assumed command of *SS-Inf.Rgt.6* and *SS-Ostubaf.* Kohlroser assumed command of *SS-Inf.Rgt.7*. By designating two highly experienced officers to command the two infantry regiments of the SS division, the *SS-FHA* hoped to improve their combat capabilities. Between July 15-30, the units of *SS-Inf.Rgt.7* took up positions in the Lampela area, setting up defensive positions. On July 21, *Nord* had 271 officers, 544 NCOs and 7,387 soldiers. During the course of the month of July, another 33 officers and 200 NCOs arrived as reinforcements.

Bibliography

M. Afiero, "*The 6th Waffen-SS Gebirgs (Mountain) Division Nord*", Schiffer Publishing
F. Schreiber, "*Kampf unter dem Nordlich*", Munin Verlag 1969
C.Trang, "*Dictionnaire de la Waffen SS, volume I*", Editions Heimdal

A review of Italian SS collar patches

by Hugh Page Taylor

A recruiting poster painted for the Italian SS Legion by the artist Gino Boccasile.

Preamble

A lot has been written about the Italian SS and considerable progress has been made over the years in our understanding of their history, organization and insignia. Not much was known by the Italian Army of the South as late as December 1944 and what was known was in large part inaccurate. After a period of little progress, it was not until 1967 that details first became available when Giorgio Pisanò published his sympathetic monumental 2,390 page history of the armed forces of the RSI, 48 of which were devoted to the 29th Italian SS Division. This was followed 15 years later in 1982 by the first book devoted entirely to the subject, the highly critical 398-page *"Le SS Italiane"* ("The Italian SS") by Ricciotti Lazzero (see bibliography). Without question, the greatest progress by far was made another 13 years later by two Italian historians who under pseudonyms in 2001 published a detailed 430-page history of the Italian SS Legion, which no-one seriously interested in this subject should be without: *"Sentire – Pensare – Volere"* (see bibliography). These and a number of articles mainly in American periodicals have described in detail the uniforms and insignia worn by the Italian SS, correcting some errors, yet creating others. One of the more interesting debates has been over what was surely the rarest, most unusual and distinctive of all SS badges, the so-called *"3 arrows"* collar patch, known more correctly as the *"3 arrows and yoke"*. Thanks to the testimony of veterans of the Italian SS, such as former *Waffen-Ostuf.* Prof. Pio Filippani-Ronconi, research by experts on the subject such as Marco Novarese and Fausto Sparacino and collectors like the late Alessandro Raspagni, fresh and exciting information and photographs have come to light that have added to our knowledge and answered some of the outstanding questions – yet at the same time

Italian *Waffen-SS* troops on the march through Northern Italy (*Corbatti-Nava Collection*).

British POWs near Nettuno, February 1944 (BA).

have raised others and, in some cases, caused a degree of confusion. The purpose of this article is first to examine what is known and then consider the questions that remain unanswered. However, the most important and unquestionably reliable information given below comes thanks to the untiring efforts of who has been this author's best friend in Italy since 1973, *Arch.* (= architect) Carlo Castellina, one of the great characters of Italian militaria collecting and research for some five decades. Through his friendship with the late Vittorio Lorioli, Carlo found original and unique documentation concerning the SS insignia made in 1944 by the firm Lorioli's grandfather founded in 1919, in particular the *"3 arrows"* collar badge. Before examining this documentation, however, let us look back at what we knew of the badge before this discovery.

Italian SS collar patches

One characteristic of Italian SS insignia was that rank was at first shown on both left and right collar patches, but the truly unique feature was that, although based on the German system, with rank indicated by bars, stars and oak leaves, the base color of the patches was red, not the usual SS black. Both of these features changed in recognition of the *"valor and sense of duty"* demonstrated by the Italian SS at the Anzio/Nettuno bridgehead, during Operation *Shingle*. The Allies landed on 22 January 1944 on Italy's western coast some 55km (35 miles) south of Rome and an Italian SS battle group performed well and suffered severe losses after it reached the front in March. Karl Wolff, who was not only the Highest SS and Police Leader in Italy (*Der Höchste SS- und Polizeiführer Italien*), but also the Supreme Commander (*Il Comandante Supremo*) of what

SS-Obergruppenführer und General der Waffen-SS **Karl Wolff, wearing the EKI and Golden Party Badge he was awarded in 1918 and on 30 January 1939 respectively (*Photograph courtesy the late Mark Yerger*).**

were called in March and April 1944 the *"Italian Volunteer Legion"* (*Legione Volontari Italiani*), and by 10 June 1944 the *"Italian Armed Units of the SS"* (*Unità Armate Italiane delle SS*), otherwise generically referred to as the *"Italian SS Legion"* (*Legione SS Italiana*), had sought authorization for recognition of the efforts, bravery and sacrifice of the Italian SS from the head of the SS, Heinrich Himmler in Berlin(1). Wolff's request was successful and led to the *Reichsführer-SS* (RFSS) making two announcements: on 3 May 1944 that the Italian SS volunteers were to be considered members of the *Waffen-SS* with all the duties and rights this involved, and on 15 June 1944, that they were to wear badges of rank and other insignia on a black backing, just the same as the men of the other SS units(2).

Oblong rather than parallelogram patches?

As seen above, the first detailed study of the Italian SS to be published was in Giorgio Pisanò's 1967 illustrated history of the armed forces of the Italian Social Republic: *"Gli Ultimi in Grigio Verde"* subtitled *"Storia delle Forze Armate della R.S.I."* Although incredibly detailed for the period in which it was written, it did contain errors, a number of which concerned the collar patches worn by the Italian SS. One of these was to show in drawings by Piero Baldrati on pages 715/718 the left and right patches to have been oblong in shape, rather than the correct paralellograms. This may be deemed inexcusable given the numerous historical photographs included in the study, but may have been influenced by the same error made in February 1945 in a secret report published by the Information Office of the General Headquarters of the Italian Co-belligerant Army (*Esercito Cobelligerante Italiano*) or Army of the South (*Esercito del Sud*), which from October 1943 was allowed to fight alongside the Allies in the liberation of its country. The report was called "Situation of Occupied Italy" (*Situazione dell'Italia Occupata*"), was an attachment to the "Information Bulletin" (*Bollettino Informazione*) number 460 of 3 February 1945, and was based on information considered valid up to 31 December 1944.

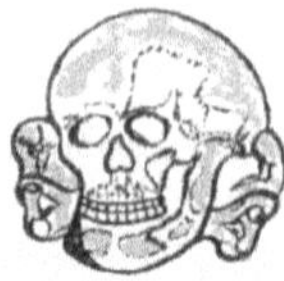

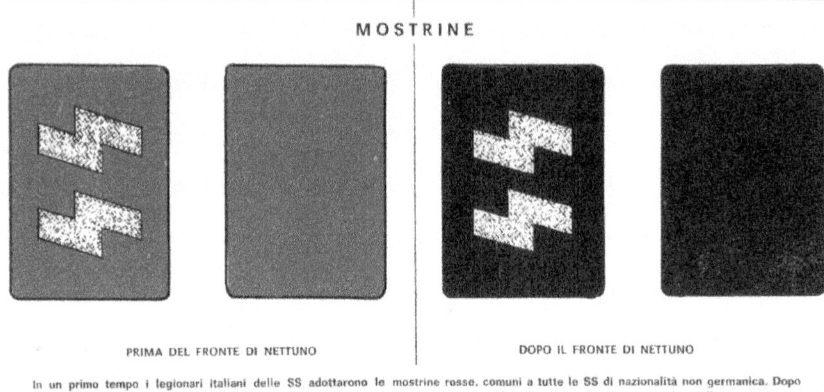

Plate appearing on page 715 of Pisanò's trilogy *"Gli Ultimi in Grigio Verde"* and serialised as *"Storia delle Forze Armate della R.S.I."* showing a pair of rectangular collar patches, red at left and black at right. The caption states that *"At first the Italian SS legionnaires adopted red collar patches, in common with all the non-Germanic SS..."* which is incorrect, as such was only the case with Italians.

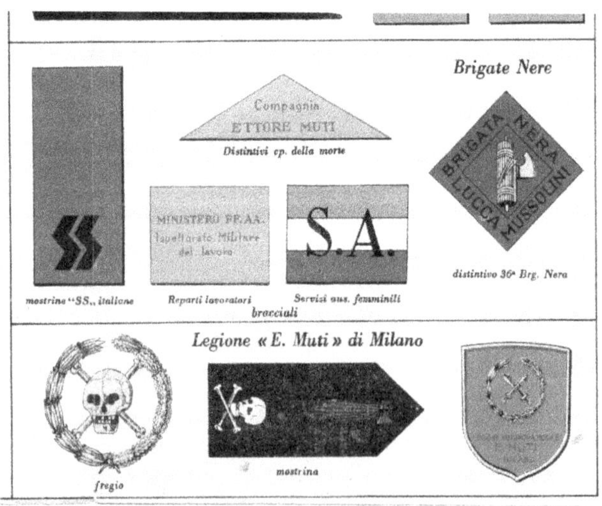

Part of the plate forming Attachment 1 to the February 1945 *"Situation of Occupied Italy"* based on information gathered and so considered valid upto the end of 1944, showing at top left a fantasy collar patch with incorrectly drawn black SS runes on a non-existant elongated rectangular red collar patch (*Author's collection*).

Among the errors was to list two rather than one Italian SS division(3), but that pertinent to this study was to depict the collar patch of the Italian SS in attachment 1. This had totally incorrectly drawn black SS runes on a long rectrangular red patch: apart from steel helmet decals, when the Siegrunen were worn they were white or silver, not black, and red collar patches had been replaced by black long before the end of 1944.

Left, a pair of questionably original rectangular black collar patches below an Italian SS sleeve eagle. The two bars indicate a *Waffen-Rottenführer*. Right, a matching pair of questionably original rectangular collar patches for a *Waffen-Scharführer*.

It is true that unofficial insignia were worn by the Italian SS, such as hand-made SS runes on black and red collar patches, but no historical photographs have so far been found of any rectangular patches being worn. Some exist, but whether they were made prior to the end of WW2 or some time since is not known.

Left, a *Waffen-Untersturmführer* wearing what appear to have been regular black SS collar patches with the SS runes. Right, a *Waffen-Sturmmann* wearing what appear to be hand-made black collar patches with SS runes (*Courtesy Franco Mesturini*).

Der Reichsführer-SS
RF/M. 35/42/44

Feld-Kommandostelle, den 4. Mai 1944

An
1. Chef des SS-Führungshauptamtes
2. Chef des SS-Hauptamtes.

Alle italienischen Angehörigen unserer SS-Divisionen haben mit sofortiger Wirksamkeit

1. den Spiegel für italienische Waffenwillige,
2. das italienische Landesschild

zu tragen.

Diese Maßnahme ist beschleunigt durchzuführen.

gez. H. Himmler -

3. Höchsten SS- und Polizeiführer Italien
4. SS-Brigadeführer Fegelein
5. SS-Oberführer Rode
6. SS-Sturmbannführer Grothmann

durchschriftlich mit der Bitte um Kenntnisnahme übersandt.

Brandt
SS-Standartenführer

Himmler's order of 4 May 1944.

Nur für den Dienstgebrauch

Verordnungsblatt der Waffen-SS
(V. Bl. d. W.-SS)
Herausgegeben vom SS-Führungshauptamt, Berlin-Wilmersdorf, Kaiserallee 188

5. Jahrgang | Berlin, den 15. April 1944 | Nummer 8

Page 49 (front cover) of the "*Verordnungsblatt der Waffen-SS*", No. 8, 15 April 1944.

Wolff relayed the RFSS's order concerning the black collar patches in his Order of the Day (*Tagesbefehl*) No. 65, which was published in the Italian SS newspaper "*Avanguardia*" on 20 May 1944, anticipating that a special badge would be introduced for wear on the right hand side collar patch. No details were given (and it is not true that the "*3 arrows*" badge was officially sanctioned by Wolff in his Day Order No. 65 of May 1944,(4)) and it appears that the intention at that stage was for such a badge to be worn only by those members of the Italian SS who had served at the front. So at some time after the middle of June 1944 the red collar patches were replaced by black and, in anticipation of the introduction of the mystery badge for the right side of the collar, rank was no longer worn on both patches, and plain black right hand patches were worn, or those with SS runes. But mystery surrounds the design of the badge selected for wear on the right patch and, apart from plain black and the SS runes, there were two possibilities.

Littorian fasces (Fascio Littorio)

On 4 May 1944, Himmler ordered from his field headquarters that with immediate effect Italian members of SS divisions were to wear "the collar patch for Italian volunteers" (*den Spiegel für italienische Waffenwillige*)(5). While the design of such a collar patch was not given in that order, there is no doubt that Himmler's original intention was for Italian volunteers in the *Waffen-SS* to wear an embroidered Littorian fasces (*Fascio Littorio* in Italian and *Liktorenbundel* in German) manufactured in Germany (presumably at Dachau), and his order was published by the 1st Staff Officer of the SS Main Operational Office (*Ia SS-Führungshauptamt*) on 15 April 1944, with the badge to be manufactured under reference

166. Herstellung von Filmen über die Waffen-SS.

1. Für die Herstellung von Filmen in der und über die Waffen-SS ist die SS-Standarte „Kurt Eggers" ausschließlich zuständig.

2. Anträge zur Durchführung von Filmvorhaben sind an die SS-Standarte „Kurt Eggers" direkt zu richten.

3. Über die Durchführung von Filmvorhaben entscheidet nach Unterrichtung durch die SS-Standarte „Kurt Eggers" das SS-Führungshauptamt.

SS-FHA Ia

167. Kragenspiegel für Freiwillige in der Waffen-SS dienende Italiener.

Der Reichsführer-SS hat für die italienischen Freiwilligen bei der Waffen-SS einen rechtsseitig mit dem Liktorenbündel bestickten Kragenspiegel genehmigt. Auf dem linken Kragenspiegel werden, wie bei allen Angehörigen der Waffen-SS, die Dienstgradabzeichen getragen.

Bezeichnung:

Kragenspiegel m. Liktorenbündel . . . Art.Nr. B 771

Die Einheiten und Dienststellen fordern den Bedarf auf dem Bekleidungsnachschubwege an.

SS-FHA Ia

168. Erfassung von Spitzenkönnern im Schießen.

Die gemäß H.V.Bl. vom 15. 3. 1944 unter Ziffer 63 zu erstattende Meldung von Spitzenkönnern im Schießen gilt auch für die Waffen-SS.

Meldungen sind nach vorgeschriebenem Muster bis 1. Mai 1944 an SS-FHA Id zu erstatten.

SS-FHA Id

169. Urlaubssperre nach Ostrumänien.

Der Urlaub nach Transnistrien, Buchenland und Bessarabien wird mit sofortiger Wirkung gesperrt.

SS-FHA Amt II Ic

170. Beurlaubung nach Rumänien.

I.

Der Reichsführer-SS hat befohlen, daß jeder Urlaub nach Rumänien, der über 21 Tage hinausgeht, seiner Entscheidung bedarf. Anträge sind über SS-FHA Amt II Ic einzureichen.

Darüber hinaus hat der Reichsführer-SS befohlen, daß jeder Urlauber vor Antritt des Urlaubs zu belehren ist, daß er sich in keine politischen Dinge einmischen darf, und daß er sich am ersten Tage seines Aufenthaltes in Rumänien bei der zuständigen Ortsgruppe der Volksgruppenführung zu melden hat.

Die Pflicht zur Meldung bei der nächsten deutschen militärischen Dienststelle bzw. bei der SS-Ers.Insp. Südostraum, Dienststelle Rumänien in Kronstadt, bleibt weiterhin bestehen.

II.

Es wird erneut darauf hingewiesen, daß in Rumänien beheimatete Freiwillige der Waffen-SS jährlich höchstens 30 Urlaubstage in Rumänien verbringen dürfen.

Nach einer mit dem Kgl.Rum. Großen Generalstab getroffenen Vereinbarung gilt für die Beurlaubung nach Rumänien das Kalenderjahr.

SS-FHA Amt II Ic

171. Meldung über unerlaubte Entfernung und Fahnenflucht.

Für Meldungen über unerlaubte Entfernung und Fahnenflucht sind in Zukunft Vordrucke zu verwenden. Bezug nur durch Verlag W. F. Mayr, Miesbach (Obb.), Bestell-Nr. W.-SS 8501.

SS-FHA Amt II Ic

172. Feldpostprüfung.

Ab sofort ist die von im Ausland beheimateten Freiwilligen der Waffen-SS aufgegebene Post, sofern sich Absender und Empfänger im Reichsgebiet befinden, nicht mehr über eine SS-Feldpostprüfstelle zu leiten. Ziffer 5 der Verfügung V.Bl.d.W.-SS vom 1. 3. 1944 Nr. 106 ist entsprechend abzuändern.

SS-FHA Amt II Ic

173. Einreichung von Fahndungsanzeigen an die SS-Ersatzkommandos; hier: Berichtigung zur Veröffentlichung im V.Bl.d.W.-SS vom 1. 4. 1944 Nr. 146.

1. In der zweiten Zeile muß es heißen: . . . sind in Zukunft auf direktem Wege in einer Durchschrift auch an das zuständige SS-Ersatzkommando einzusenden.

2. Im 2. Absatz:

Allen Staaten Südosteuropas:

SS-Ersatz-Inspektion „Südostraum"
Wien 13, Gloriettegasse 14/16

dazu einen weiteren Durchschlag an:

Ungarn
Dienststelle Feldpostnummer 04 345 E

Slowakei
Dienststelle Feldpostnummer 01 981 B

Kroatien
Dienststelle Feldpostnummer 03 161 B

— 50 —

Page 50 of the *"Verordnungsblatt der Waffen-SS"*, No. 8, 15 April 1944, with item 167 headed *"Collar patch for Italian volunteers serving in the Waffen-SS"*.

"Article B 771"(6). The Littorian fasces was the second symbol of the National Fascist Party (*Partito Nazionale Fascista,* or PNF) and consisted of a bundle of rods with an axe blade protruding from the side, and the contemporary references to it as an SS collar patch found so far are:

a) 15 April 1944: Himmler's above-cited order of that date

b) 4 May 1944: idem

c) 15 November 1944: Illustration captioned *"Italien"* in a 1945 Danish SS pocket calendar that went to press on this date(7).

d) 1 February 1945: Map of arm shields and collar patches of the non-German units of the *Waffen-SS,* as at this date, produced by the SS Planning Unit of the SS Main Office(8).

That such a patch was actually manufactured is proven by examples that have been found in collections since soon after the war.

Liktorenbundel collar patch, as illustrated and/or described between 15 April 1944 and 1 February 1945 for Italians serving in the *Waffen-SS,* which was manufactured in Germany but never in fact worn. This image is taken from the 1945 Danish pocket calendar.

That is certainly powerful evidence that such a design was intended, and most of the other collar patches shown on the SS-FHA map have been found in contemporary photographs (and in some documents) to have been introduced and worn. But while Himmler did order that particular style of fasces and it was certainly manufactured, to the best of this author's knowledge not a single photograph has ever been found proving it was in fact worn before the end of the war(9). One reason is surely that the *Fascio di Littorio* (as described above) was associated with the first period of Italian fascist

Section of the 1 February 1945 SS Main Office map showing the Liktorenbundel for Italy.

government, which of course came to an end on 25 July 1943 with a vote of no confidence by the Grand Council of Fascism, Mussolini's arrest and the dissolution of the PNF. But the Italian SS came into being during the second period, the tragic, claustrophobic Italian Social Republic (*Repubblica Sociale Italiana,* or RSI), which came into being more as a collaborationist regime than an ally of Germany, and to distinguish itself had the so-called republican fasces (*Fascio Repubblicano*) as its symbol, which had been the first fascist badge from 1919 to 1923 and had the axe head attached to the rod running up along the centre of the bundle of rods and which protruded from the top, not the side. Logically, the republican fasces should have been chosen for the right hand Italian SS collar patch to match the unique sleeve eagle, but such was not the case. In fact no specific symbol appears to have been worn from the birth of what would become the Italian SS until December 1944, with patches showing rank, SS runes and with no emblem at all until then.

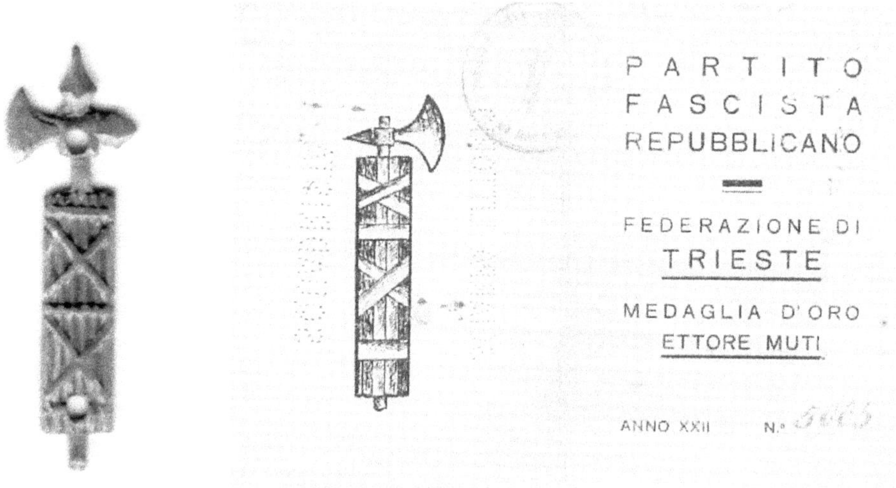

Republican fasces, the fascist symbol first from 1919 to 1923 (represented here at left by a metal device from the left side of the grip of a 1923 model Fascist Militia dagger, carried until 1935) and then of the RSI from 1943 to 1945 (here at right printed on the rear of a provisional membership card for the Trieste Federation of the Republican Fascist Party for the XXIIst Year of the Fascist Era, that is from 29 October 1943 to 28 October 1944).

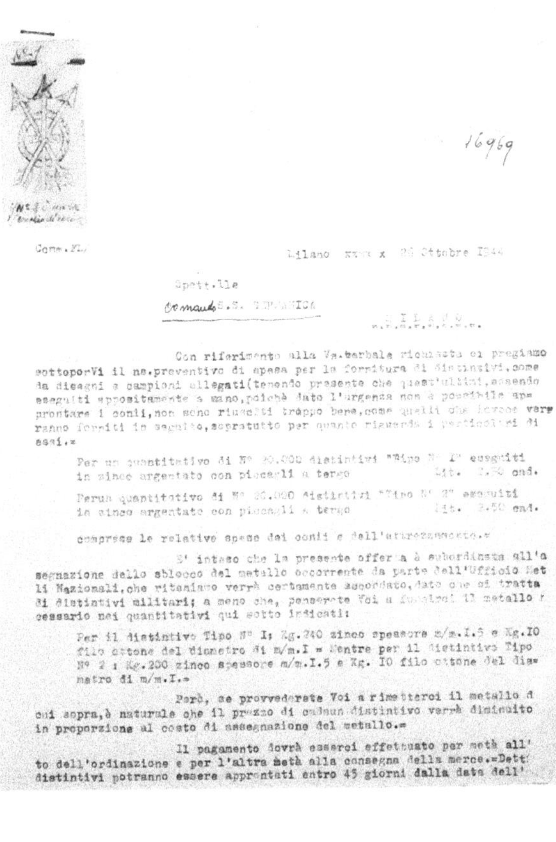

16969

Comm. FL/

Milano [illegible] x 26 Ottobre 1944

Spett.lle
Comando S.S. [illegible]
M I L A N O

Con riferimento alla Vs. verbale richiesta ci pregiamo sottoporVi il ns. preventivo di spesa per la fornitura di distintivi, come da disegni e campioni allegati (tenendo presente che quest'ultimi, essendo eseguiti appositamente a mano, poichè dato l'urgenza non è possibile approntare i conii, non sono riusciti troppo bene, come quelli che invece verranno forniti in seguito, sopratutto per quanto riguarda i particolari di essi.=

Per un quantitativo di N° 20.000 distintivi "Tipo N° I" eseguiti in zinco argentato con piccagli a tergo Lit. [illegible] cad.

Per un quantitativo di N° 20.000 distintivi "Tipo N° 2" eseguiti in zinco argentato con piccagli a tergo Lit. [illegible].50 cad.

comprese le relative spese dei conii e dell'attrezzamento.=

E' inteso che la presente offerta è subordinata all'assegnazione dello sblocco del metallo occorrente da parte dell'Ufficio Metalli Nazionali, che riteniamo verrà certamente accordato, dato che si tratta di distintivi militari; a meno che, penserete Voi a fornirci il metallo necessario nei quantitativi qui sotto indicati:

Per il distintivo Tipo N° I; Kg. 240 zinco spessore m/m. I.5 e Kg. IO filo ottone del diametro di m/m. I = Mentre per il distintivo Tipo N° 2: Kg. 200 zinco spessore m/m. I.5 e Kg. IO filo ottone del diametro di m/m. I.=

Però, se provvederete Voi a rimetterci il metallo di cui sopra, è naturale che il prezzo di cadaun distintivo verrà diminuito in proporzione al costo di assegnazione del metallo.=

Il pagamento dovrà esserci effettuato per metà all'atto dell'ordinazione e per l'altra metà alla consegna della merce.= Detti distintivi potranno essere approntati entro 45 giorni dalla data dell'

SEGUITO LETTERA

[illegible]ne.=

Il predetto preventivo dovrà però essere sottoposto all'approvazione della ns. Direzione che attualmente è [illegible] in Bergamo, ed in base a quanto essa disporrà, il presente potrà essere [illegible] valido.=

Restiamo quindi in attesa di Vs. comunicazioni al riguardo e nel frattempo, ringraziandoVi, ben distintamente Vi salutiamo.=

[illegible]

Lorioli's draft letter dated 26 October 1944. The "Received" stamp at top left is dated 1 November 1944 and bears the firm's order number: 16969.

The likely explanation is that following Himmler's order of 15 April 1944, the SS-FHA instructed a quantity of the patches to be manufactured at the *Waffen-SS* clothing factory (*Bekleidungswerke der Waffen-SS*) in Dachau. Why they were never sent to Italy is not known, and this may have been because the Germans discovered in time that the Littorian fasces badge was not only unsuitable but also unacceptable. It is just possible that some of these were taken to Italy and may even have been worn by a few members of the Italian SS, but what is more likely is that undistributed examples found when the concentration camp and other SS installations at Dachau were liberated on 29 April 1945 were taken home as souvenirs by U.S. soldiers and ended up in collections.

The "3 arrows"

The badge that is the main subject of this analysis, which is unique in its design and until now has been little understood, was certainly manufactured in large quantities and worn. This extraordinary and most interesting item of *Waffen-SS* insignia remained unknown and so absent from the books published on the subject until 1981[10]. That was when former *Waffen-Ostuf.* Prof. Pio Filippani-Ronconi brought it to the attention of collectors by sharing an amazing photograph of him wearing it. Since then, examples of the badge – in rare cases attached to a black patch – have come onto the militaria collecting market and a few other photographs of it being worn have become available, for example in the Corbatti/Nava book (see bibliography).

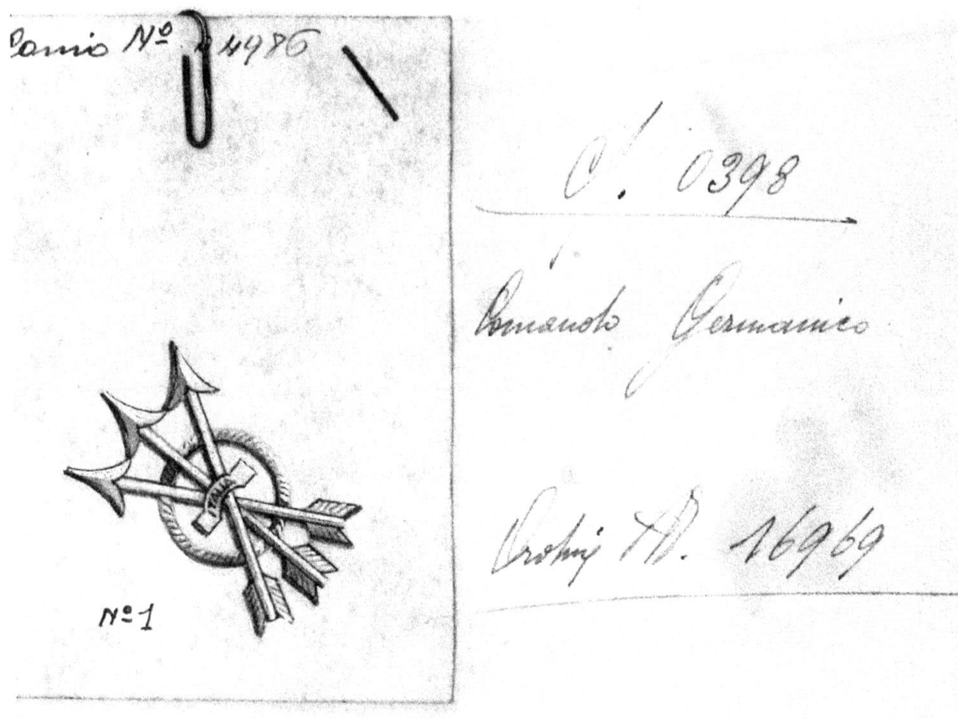

Lorioli's drawing of the "3 arrows".

Sample "3 arrows" badge on its Lorioli sample card.

With one exception, no precise dates were, however, given for any of these photographs and what now appear to have been guesses were published by "experts" identifying the badge as having been intended for and worn only by specific units of the Italian SS, not the organisation as a whole. As will be seen below, documents Carlo Castellina has come up with go a long way to documenting this extraordinary badge, especially as to the timeline of its short life, and its intended distribution. But before examining that documentation and the information it contains, the symbolism of the badge's design and how it may have come to be selected for the Italian SS need to be considered. The badge was chosen by a number of Italian SS officers who believed in anthroposophy (*antroposofia* in Italian), a word meaning "*wisdom of the human being*", or "*awareness of one's humanity"*[11]. Such is said to have had a following amongst the uppermost circles of the SS in Germany, and to have been a characteristic of the Wewelburg castle, Himmler's SS *"shrine"*. According to Filippani-Ronconi via Novarese[12], a group of senior Italian SS officers, including *Waffen-Hauptsturmführer* Leale Martelli, who visited Wewelsburg in 1944, and *Waffen-Sturmbannführer* Asvero Gravelli, the arrow was considered one of the more important symbols and the entire castle at Wewelsburg was built in the shape of one. It is beyond the scope of this article to confirm this, but the plan of the castle was in fact a triangle, at best an arrow head, not an arrow[13].

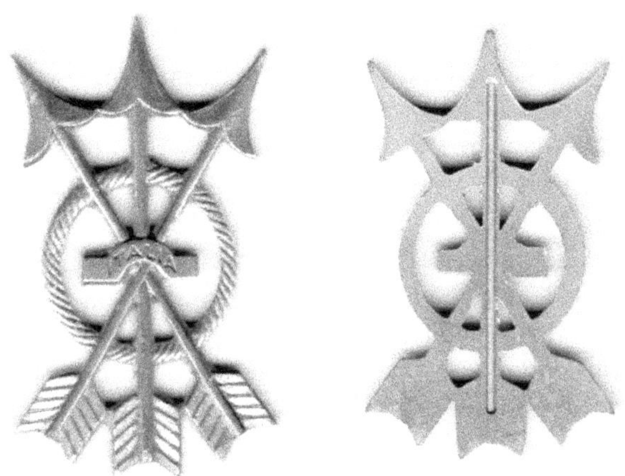

Left, obverse of the "3 arrows and yoke" badge. Right, Reverse of a "3 arrows and yoke" badge. This example is unfinished in that the wire prong fastening has not been inserted in the central vertical slot. It is therefore either an unfinished example surplus to the 20,000 requirement, or a post-war example made from the original mould.

From the left, *SS-Oberfiihrer* Erich Tschimpke, *Sturmbannfiihrer* Asvero Gravelli, *Generalmajor* Piero Mannelli and *SS-Sturmbannfuhrer* Luis Thaler.

Filippani-Ronconi is also claimed to have said that the yoke and three arrows had a special meaning in anthroposophy, the arrows the three principal human functions of *das Denken – das Fühlen – das Wollen* (think, feel, will) and the yoke the medium that unifies the three arrows/functions, and that it was Martelli and his fellow officers of the Press and Propaganda Detachment of the Italian SS Legion who chose these devices for the collar badge of their organization[14]. According to this version, the German *SS-Oberführer* Erich Tschimpke[15] and the Italian Inspector General of the Italian SS, *Waffen-Brigadeführer und Generalmajor der SS* Piero Mannelli[16], approved this design, as did the Highest SS and Police Leader and Commander of the *Waffen-SS* in Italy Karl Wolff, who submitted it to *Reichsführer-SS* Heinrich Himmler for his approval.

F. M. Lorioli Fratelli

The firm that bore the name of the Lorioli family was formed in 1919 by the brothers Filippo

and Michele Lorioli (the "F." and "M." in the company name), who originally worked out of modest premises in Via Francesco Anzani 3 in Milan. Their original activity as an "artistic establishment" (*Stabilimento Artistico*) was primarily to manufacture WWI commemorative medals, but their production was expanded at first to produce sports medals and then, after Mussolini assumed control after the March on Rome of 28 October 1922, grew dramatically in an Italy dominated by Fascist uniforms, medals and badges. Such was the growth following Mussolini's assumption of power that in 1923 the firm was obliged to move to new and larger premises at Via Bronzetti 25 in Milan, which was not only the company's head office, but also housed the workshop and the Lorioli family. These premises were badly damaged in an Allied air raid in August 1943, but production continued, also with a branch in Rome at Via delle Carrozze 3. In all, the Lorioli firm produced over 40,000 different moulds for medals and in excess of 20,000 moulds for badges, signs and similar items. Although no longer active, Via Bronzetti 25 was kept on after the war as a sort of office museum, housing the fabulous "Lorioli Archive".

From September 1943 until the end of the war in Italy in late April 1945, Lorioli received orders from the occupying Germans, to include a number of badges for the Italian SS. These can be considered in two distinct groups, according to the period the badges were ordered, manufactured and delivered, and the German authority that chose Lorioli as manufacturer:

- Between late January and 9 May 1944, Branch 12 of the *Wehrmacht* Procurement Office (*Wehrmacht Beschaffungsamt, Zweigstelle 12*) in Via Tonale 2, Milan, placed orders with Lorioli for a) 20,000 SS death's head cap badges on behalf of the H.Q. of the Armed Militia (*Kommando Milizia Armata*), which by the beginning of March 1944 had been redesignated *Kdo.-Stab Ital. Freiw.Legionen*; b) 34,500 large rank pips for shoulder straps (33,000 colored silver, 1,500 gold); c) 10,000 small rank pips for collar patches; and d) 20,000 Italian SS cap badges with the eagle clutching a Republican fasces in its talons (700 of these were destined for the "Milan Battalion", translated by Lorioli as the Ist Battalion of Italian Volunteers (*I° Battaglione Volontari Italiani*);

- On 5 November 1944, the Highest SS and Police Leader "Italy" and Commander in Chief of the *Waffen-SS* (*Der Höchste SS und Polizeiführer "Italien" Der Befehlshaber der Waffen-SS*) ordered 20,000 of the "3 arrows" device for the right hand collar patch.

The information that follows was given to Carlo Castellina by his friend Vittorio Lorioli, grandson of the founding partner Filippo.

***SS-Obergruppenführer* Karl Wolff.**

Manufacture of the "3 arrows and yoke"

At some time in October 1944 Lorioli received an urgent telephone call from what they noted at the time as "The German SS Command" (*Comando S.S. Germanica*), which in fact turned out to be the office of the Highest SS and Police Leader "Italy" – the Commander of the *Waffen-SS* (*Der Höchste SS und Polizeiführer "Italien" - Der Befehlshaber der Waffen-SS*). This was the headquarters of Karl Wolff, *SS-Obergruppenführer und General der Waffen-SS* who, apart from being the Highest SS and Police Leader and Commander of the *Waffen-SS* in that part of Italy not yet liberated by the Allies, was also the formal Supreme Commander of the Italian SS. Wolff's H.Q. was in the Caldiero Municipality of the Province of Verona in the Veneto Region, some 56 miles (90 km) west of Venice and 9 miles (15 km) east of Verona. Its Field Post Number used in correspondence with Lorioli for security reasons was 44190[17]. Lorioli's employee took careful note of the German's detailed request, to provide an urgent quotation for two versions of a new badge:

Type 1: a cluster of 3 arrows pointing upwards, superimposed over a rope ring and with a yoke bearing the word "ITALIA" superimposed over the junction of the arrows in the centre of the ring. It is to be noted that Lorioli referred to the badge as both "*3 arrows with yoke and Italia* ring" (*tre frecce con giogo e cerchio "Italia"*) and "*arrows – yoke and ring*" (*frecce – giogo e cerchio*).

Type 2: as Type 1, but without the rope ring.

Lorioli drafted a reply in Italian dated 26 October 1944, which may well have been translated into German, but only a carbon copy of the original has been found. Attached to this draft were two drawings of the badges. The letter provided the firm's best quotation for the badges, attaching sketches and samples. Insofar as the samples were concerned, the letter pointed out that urgency had not allowed dies to be made and so the badges had had to be made by hand and so had not "*turned out too well*", which would not be the case with those they would supply if given the order, which would also have far better detail. A unit price of Lit. (= Italian lire) 2.50 was quoted for both versions of the badge, on the basis of an order of 20,000 pieces made of silvered zinc. This price included the costs of producing the die and tooling. The badges would come fitted with fastenings (*piccagli*) on the reverse. Technical details followed, along with the caveat that the offer was subject to approval by the National Metals Office for the allocation of the metal required to manufacture the badges, such being 240 or 200 kilos of 1.5mm thick zinc for types 1 and 2 respectively and 10 kilos of 1.00mm diameter brass wire for both types. As for payment and delivery, half of the quoted price would be due when the order was confirmed and the other half upon delivery of the badges, such could be 45 days after confirmation of the order. The letter closed by noting that this quotation still had to be approved by the company's managers, who were at that time in Bergamo.

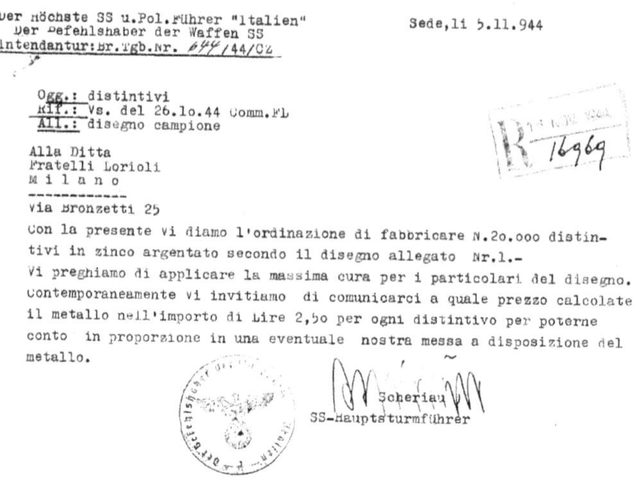

Der Höchste SS u.Pol.Führer "Italien"
Der Befehlshaber der Waffen SS
Intendantur:Br.Tgb.Nr. 644/44/Cz

Sede,li 5.11.944

Ogg.: distintivi
Rif.: Vs. del 26.10.44 Comm.FL
All.: disegno campione

R 16969

Alla Ditta
Fratelli Lorioli
M i l a n o

Via Bronzetti 25

Con la presente vi diamo l'ordinazione di fabbricare N.20.000 distintivi in zinco argentato secondo il disegno allegato Nr.1.-
Vi preghiamo di applicare la massima cura per i particolari del disegno. Contemporaneamente vi invitiamo di comunicarci a quale prezzo calcolate il metallo nell'importo di Lire 2,50 per ogni distintivo per poterne conto in proporzione in una eventuale nostra messa a disposizione del metallo.

Scheriau
SS-Hauptsturmführer

***SS-Hstuf.* Scheriau's letter of 5 November 1944, confirming the order for 20,000 Type 1 "3 arrows" badges.**

SS-Hauptsturmführer Hans Scheriau of the quartermaster general's department of the Commander of the *Waffen-SS* in Italy replied on 5 November 1944(18), confirming the order for 20,000 badges of Type 1 (i.e. with the rope ring).

Dir./LE 0398

15 Novembre 1944

CONFERMA D'ORDINE Nº 16969
=.=.=.=.=.=.=.=.=.=.=.=.=.=.=.

Spett.
COMANDO GERMANICO
DER HOSHESTE SS.U.POL.FUHRER "ITALIEN"
DER BEFEHLSHABER DER WAFFEN SS. = INTENDANTUR
BR.TGB.Nº644-44-CZ?

Riferendoci al pregiato Vs/.ordine conferitoci di presenza a mezzo vs/.incaricato,ci pregiamo confermarlo come segue :

Conio : Tre frecce con giogo e cerchio "Italia" nº04986/D

20.000 distintivi in zinco argentato con piccagli a tergo; al prezzo di : cadauno Lit.2.50

come da vs/.disegno.

PAGAMENTO : Lit.25.000.= anticipate; saldo per contanti a vista fattura.

CONSEGNA : al più presto possibile.

SPEDIZIONE A MEZZO : Vs/.incaricato che passerà per il ritiro.

Distinti saluti.=

F.M.LORIOLI FRATELLI

Lorioli's letter of 15 November 1944 to Wolff's office confirming the order.

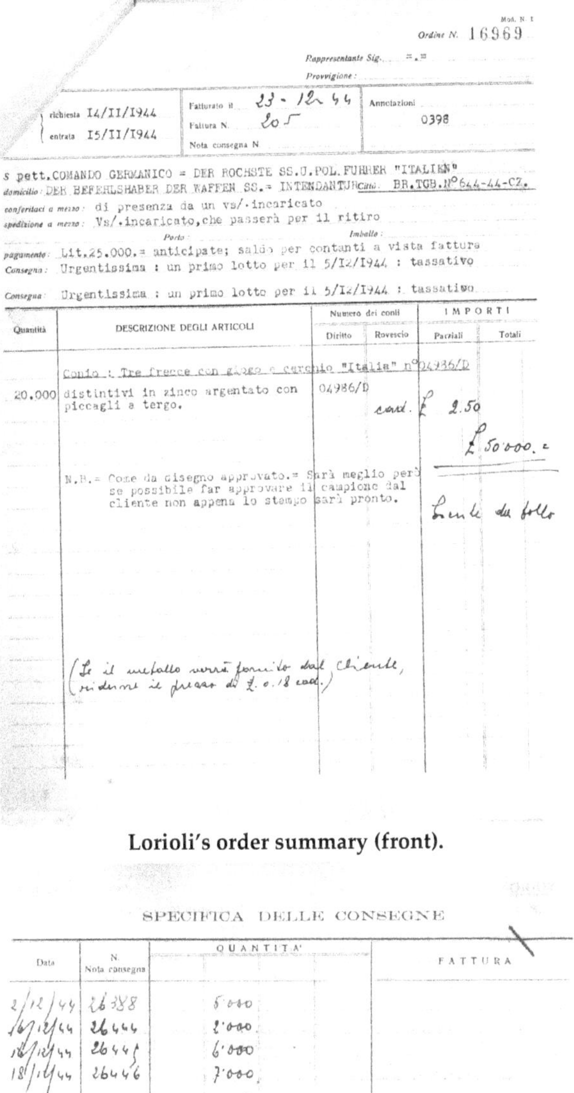

Mod. N. 1

Ordine N. 16969

Rappresentante Sig. =.=

Provvigione:

richiesta I4/II/1944 entrata I5/II/1944	Fatturato il 23-12-44 Fattura N. 205 Nota consegna N.	Annotazioni 0398

s pett. COMANDO GERMANICO = DER ROCHSTE SS.U.POL.FUHRER "ITALIEN"
domicilio: DER BEFEHLSHABER DER WAFFEN SS.= INTENDANTUR Città: BR.TGB.N°644-44-CZ.
conferitaci a mezzo: di presenza da un vs/.incaricato
spedizione a mezzo: Vs/.incaricato, che passerà per il ritiro
Porto: Imballo:
pagamento: Lit.25.000.= anticipate; saldo per contanti a vista fattura
Consegna: Urgentissima : un primo lotto per il 5/I2/1944 : tassativo
Consegna: Urgentissima : un primo lotto per il 5/I2/1944 : tassativo

Quantità	DESCRIZIONE DEGLI ARTICOLI	Numero dei coni – Diritto	Numero dei coni – Rovescio	IMPORTI – Parziali	IMPORTI – Totali
	Conio : Tre frecce con giogo e cerchio "Italia" n°04986/D				
20.000	distintivi in zinco argentato con piccagli a tergo.	04986/D	cad.	£ 2.50	
					£ 50.000.=
	N.B.= Come da disegno approvato.= Sarà meglio però se possibile far approvare il campione dal cliente non appena lo stampo sarà pronto.				

(Se il metallo verrà fornito dal Cliente, ridurre il prezzo di £. 0.18 [illegible].)

Lorioli's order summary (front).

SPECIFICA DELLE CONSEGNE

Data	N. Nota consegna	QUANTITA'	FATTURA
2/12/44	26388	5000	
16/12/44	26444	2000	
16/12/44	26445	6000	
18/12/44	26446	7000	

Lorioli's order summary (reverse with details).

He urged that the maximum care and attention be paid to the detail of the badges and asked what proportion of the Lit. 2.50 unit price referred to the metal, should the decision be taken for this to be supplied by the Germans to Lorioli. In the event, such was not to be the case.
The order was formalized by the usual internal documentation, to include two forms dated Milan 14 November 1944, one of which was headed "Order Copy No." and with the order No. 16969 added by hand. Lorioli's die was numbered 04986/D.

A letter was sent to Caldiero confirming the order and dated 15 November, under Lorioli's reference "Dir./LE 0398".

Lorioli's internal documentation shows that an unquantified first batch had to be delivered on 5 December. Priority was clearly given to respecting the delivery dates, and Lorioli advised their client that they could count on receiving part of the order on 1 December 1944. However, a request subsequently made in writing on 16 November that at least 1,500 badges be supplied within the 19th of that month – so as to be ready for wear at a parade to be held the following day(19) – could not be respected, and the 20,000 badges were handed over between 2 and 18 December 1944 as follows:

Delivery date	Consignment note No.	Quantity delivered
2 December 1944	26388	5,000
16 December 1944	26444	2,000
16 December 1944	26445	6,000
18 December 1944	26446	7,000
		20,000

Lorioli sent their invoice to FPNr. 44190 (Caldiero – Verona) on 23 December 1944. Once they had been distributed, the "3 arrows" badges had to be attached to the plain black right hand collar patches, possibly by men responsible for the supply of uniforms and insignia, and/or by military tailors and/or by the individual recipients themselves.

Il Comandante Supremo della SS e Pol."Italia"
Il Comandante Generale della SS
Va: Brot.Nr. 711 /44/Sche/Pa/ B-2

Sede,li 16.11.1944

Feldpost 44190
Caldiero (Verona)

Ogg.: Distintivi
rif.: Vs.nota del 26.10.1944
all.: ./.

Alla Ditta
Fratelli Lorioli
Milano
via Bronzetti 25

In data 5.11.44 questo Comando ha dato l'incarico di fabbricare 20.000 distintivi conforme l'allegato disegno ed ha fatto un acconto di Lire 25,000.=Contemporaneamente questo Comando ha avuto la notizia che a partire dal 1.12.1944 può far conto su una fornitura parziale.
Siccome per una parata del 20.11.1944 occorrono per lo meno 1500 distintivi,preghiamo di fornire ~~detto quantitativo~~ per lo meno detto quantitativo al più tardi per il 19.11.1944.
Ringraziandovi in anticipo del Vs.favore

Heil Hitler

(Scheriau)
SS-Hauptsturmführer

F.d.R.d.Ü.

SS-Hstuf. **Scheriau's letter of 16 November 1944.**

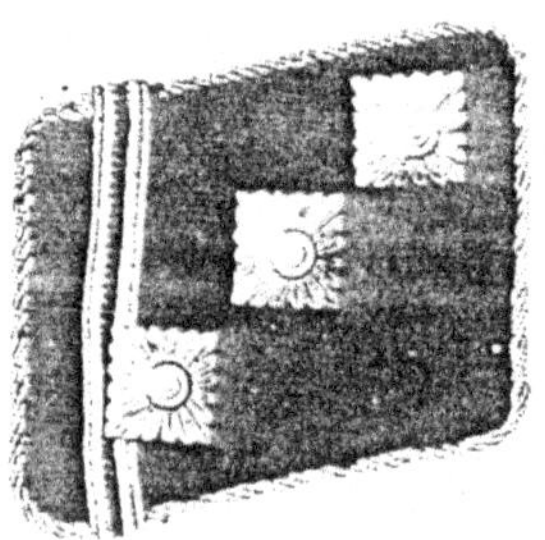

The "3 arrows" matched with a *Waffen-Obersturmführer* rank patch.

In any event, clear instructions as to how they were to be mounted were either not given or respected and they are known to have been fitted diagonally across the patch, or parallel with either the shorter or longer sides of the parallelogram. An example of an embroidered version, smaller than the regulation SS collar patch (45mm x 49mm, or 1.77" x 1.93") and not of its usual shape, is in the collection of Dr. Stefano Savino, but who manufactured it and when is not known and no historical photographs have so far been found to confirm it was ever worn.

Two pairs of matched black *Waffen-Oberstumführer* collar patches, with and without the "3 arrows" (author's collection).

***Waffen-Untersturmführer* Pio Filippani-Ronconi, wearing the "3 arrows" (mounted sideways).**

Conclusions

Was the "3 arrows" badge based on anthroposophy? Filipanni-Ronconi, surely the best qualified to answer this question, is no longer alive and we can only consider the accuracy of his statements and what we have been able to learn from the followers of anthroposophy today. First, assuming that Lorioli were the only manufacturers(20), his assertion that the "3 arrows and yoke" badges were distributed in the autumn of 1944 is inaccurate at best as the first batch was only delivered on 2 December 1944. For the same reason, his claim that the Training Battalion (*Ausbildungs-Bataillon*) received the badges at the completion of training at Rodengo-Saiano on 31 October 1944 would also appear premature.

Dates: Again, assuming that Lorioli was the first and only supplier, the earliest that the "3 arrows" could have been worn was on and after 2 December 1944. That the well-known photograph of *Waffen-Ostuf.* Graf. Pio Filippani-Ronconi was taken "around August 1944" – a fact apparently given by Filippani-Ronconi himself – would thus appear premature, unless another firm had manufactured the badge before Lorioli. Other photographs of the patch being worn are dated generically "1945" and in one recorded case specifically 17 February 1945, both therefore after Lorioli had delivered their first batch of the badges. Filippani-Ronconi's memory would therefore appear to have let him down over the "3 arrows" badge having been issued in the autumn of 1944, and specifically on 31 October of that year.

The element/s of the Italian SS that received and wore the "3 arrows": 20,000 of the badges were ordered and delivered by Lorioli in December 1944, which may be considered more than enough for the number of men in

The "3 arrows" being worn on 17 February 1945 (mounted diagonally).

The "3 arrows" being worn in early 1945 (mounted lengthwise).

the entire Italian SS, estimated at 20,000 – and certainly those who had served at the front if, as has been suggested, distribution was restricted to them(21). Consequently, reports that the "3 arrows" was intended only for specific elements, such as "the 1st Battalion of the 29th Division"(22) and "the S.S. Fusilier Bataillon "Debica" of the 29th Division"(23) are to be ignored. But for reasons as yet unknown – possibly the result of availability and/or distribution difficulties, some Italian SS units received them, while others did not. For example, according to Filippani-Ronconi via Novarese, at least the following two units were issued with black right hand collar patches, but without the "3 arrows": *6. Kp. Ausbildungs-Bataillon* and *III. Ausbildungs-Bataillon*, which became *I./WGRdSS 82* (yet *II. Ausbildungs-Bataillon*, which in February 1945 became *Waffen-Fusilier-Bataillon der SS 29*, is said to have received the "3 arrows")(24). As 20,000 of the badges had been made available by 18 December 1944, one must assume that this was the result of difficulties in getting the badges to the units, hardly a priority so late in the war.

Some questions that remain to be answered

1) Were the *Liktorenbundel* collar patches ever issued to and worn by men of the Italian SS? Evidence suggests they were not and what appeared to be such a patch being worn by an *SS-Oberscharführer* attending a lecture at the *SS-Junkerschule* Bad Tölz in 1944 in a *"Wochenschau"* newsreel on closer examination in fact turned out to be a Norwegian lion patch being worn by an officer candidate of the Norwegian Legion (*Den norske Legion*).

2) Who discovered that the *Liktorenbundel* would have been inappropriate for the RSI, and when? What correspondence was exchanged, or instructions given?

3) If the "3 arrows" were intended for all members of the Italian SS, and not just those who had served at the front or belonged to specific units, why was it not possible to deliver the badges to all elements, between 18 December and the end of the war in Italy?

Notes

(1) Wolff was born in Darmstadt on 13 May 1900 and – shortly before joining the NSDAP on 1 November 1931 as member number 695 131 – became a member of the SS with number 14 235 on 13 October of that

A supposedly genuine "3 arrows" badge, mounted on what is surely a fantasy rectangular collar patch (Fausto Sparacino, pp. 84/85 – see bibliography).

The only known example of the embroidered 3 arrows collar patch (*Courtesy Dr. Stefano Savino*).

year. He rose rapidly through the ranks of the SS, appointed as *SS-Anwärter* on 7 October 1931, *SS-Mann* on 29 October 1931, and then promoted to *SS-Scharführer* on 11 December 1931, *SS-Truppführer* on 19 January 1932, *SS-Sturmführer* – later renamed as *SS-Untersturmfuhrer* – on 18 February 1932, SS-*Sturmhauptführer* – later renamed to *SS-Hauptsturmführer* – on 30 January 1934, *SS-Sturmbannführer* on 9 November 1935, *SS-Obersturmbannführer* on 30 January 1934, *SS-Standartenführer* on 20 April 1934, *SS-Oberführer* on 4 July 1934, *SS-Brigadeführer* on 9 November 1935, and *SS-Gruppenführer* on 30 January 1937. During the war he joined the *SS-Verfügungstruppe* on 1 April 1940 and was promoted to *Generalleutnant der SS-Verfügungstruppe* on 3 May 1940, then *SS-Obergruppenführer und General der Waffen-SS* on 30 January 1942 – in addition to which he was also the Highest SS and Police Leader as well as Plenipotentiary of the German Armed Forces in Italy (*Höchster SS- und Polizei-Führer und Bevollmächtigter General der Deutschen Wehrmacht in Italien*). His final promotion to *SS-Oberst-Gruppenführer und Generaloberst der Waffen-SS* on 10 April 1945 is unconfirmed. He died in Rissenheim on 15 July 1984. The name of the Italian SS was changed a number of times. In February 1944 it was being called the *"Italian Armed Militia"* (Milizia Armata Italiana - see *"La Folgore – Periodico del VI Battaglione"*), Cuneo, Anno I, N. 6, 24 February 1944. At first its regional battalions published their own newspapers, but on 18 March 1944 the first issue of a newspaper for the whole organization appeared, *"Avanguardia"*, but it was not until issue number 3 of 1 April 1944 that the sub-heading *"The Italian SS Legion"* (La Legione SS Italiana) was added. While that generic name remained in use, Wolff authorised training manuals for the Italian SS as Supreme Commander of the Italian Volunteer Legions on 20 March 1944 (N. 005/A "Istruzione sul fucile mitragliatore Breda Mod. 30"), 23 April 1944 (N. 015: "Addestramento della Fanteria. Le fortificazioni Campali"), 25 April 1944 (007/A "Istruzione sul Mortaio da 81 mod. 35") and 25 May 1944 (N. 026: "Istruzione sul tiro contro aerei con le armi della Fanteria"), yet by 10 June 1944 the name had been changed yet again to the Italian Armed Units of the SS (N. 028: "Istruzione sugli aggressivi chimici e sulle nebbie artificiali"). The leading German military historian Dr. K.-G. Klietmann gave in his 1965 *"Die Waffen-SS eine Dokumentation"* (page 267) its German names as from February 1944 to June 1944: *1. Italienische Freiw.-Sturm-Brigade Milizia Armata (Pol.)* and *1. Sturmbrigade Italienische-Freiwilligen-Legion*, and from 7 September 1944 to April 1945: *Waffen-Grenadier-Brigade der SS (italienische Nr. 1)* and finally *29. Waffen-Grenadier-Division der SS (italienische Nr. 1)*. Wolff's Order of the Day number 65 advised that upon Hitler's orders, the Reichsführer-SS Heinrich Himmler had ordered that with effect from 27 April 1944 the 1st Assault Brigade of the Italian SS Legion (I Brigata Italiana Granatieri SS) was to be renamed as the Ist

Still from a 1944 edition of the "*Die Deutsche Wochenschau*" newsreel projected in cinemas.

Italian SS Grenadier Brigade (I Brigata Italiana Granatieri SS). That the 1st Assault Brigade of the Italian Volunteer SS Legion (*1. Sturmbrigade der italienischen freiw. Legion*) was identical to the non-Germanic *SS Grenadier Brigade (Italian Nr. 1)* (*Waffen-Grenadier-Brigade SS [italienische nr. 1]*) was confirmed in a secret telegramme sent on 14 May 1944 to the SS Economics and Administrative Head Office by *SS-Oberführer* Ernst Rode on behalf of Himmler's Headquarters Staff (*Kommandostab-Reichsführer-SS*). Confusion continued with *Waffen-Grenadier-Brigade SS – Sturmbrigade Pinerolo* given in a document dated 1 June 1944, and it was not until 7 September 1944 that the *SS-FHA* confirmed that the Milizia Armata had been renamed as *Waffen-Grenadier Brigade der SS (italienische Nr. 1)*. The unit achieved divisional status before the war ended as the *29. Waffen-Grenadier-Division der SS (ital. Nr. 1)*, but this was only on paper as at 9 April 1945 it had an overall strength of only 4,500 men and consisted of only remants of its 81st and 82nd infantry regiments and a battle group named "*Binz*".

(2) Corbatti/Nava (pseudo.), "*Sentire – Pensare – Volere: Storia della Legione SS italiana*", p. 355, state that the black collar patches were authorized after the redesignation of the Ist Assault Brigade (*I. Sturmbrigade*) to the *Waffen-Grenadier Brigade der SS* at the end of April 1944. Although this predated Himmler's order of 15 June 1944 (see Pisanò, "*Gli Ultimi in Grigioverde. Storia delle Forze Armate della Repubblica Sociale Italiana (1943 – 1945)*", Vol. 2, p. 724), it is to be noted that the introduction of the Littorian fasces badge was published on 15 April 1944 (see below). Curiously, a contemporary source on the Italian SS not only fails to give the date of Himmler's second order (15 June 1944) but also refers only to the collar patches and not the other badges ("contrassegni"): Martelli, Leale: "*La SS Formazione Politico – Militare della Nuova Europa*", April 1945, p. 46).

(3) Page 82 translates literally as follows: "*Italian "SS"*. In the same way as has been the case in the other occupied territories, immediately after the 8th of September (1943) the German authorities began to raise "Italian" SS formations. At first they made up the Armed Italian Militia (Milizia Armata Italiana, or M.A.I.) which by November 1943 had reached a total strength of about 10,000 men organised in 11 battalions under the command of general Hansen (in fact *SS-Brigadefhrer und Generalmajor der Waffen-SS* - since 30 January 1942 - Peter Hansen, born Santiago, Chile, 30 November 1896, SS number 129 846). The first 4 battalions, formed in Germany from personnel coming from concentration camps, were formed in Italy into the 1st M.I.A. Regiment (commander Consul – Paolo - De Maria), with its headquarters in Milan and subsequently in Pinerolo; the other battalions remained autonomous. The Ist and IInd battalions took part in the spring of 1944 in combat on the southern Italian front, suffering heavy losses. Subsequently the M.A.I. took on the name "*Italian Volunteer Legion*" (Legione Volontari Italiani) or "Italian SS Legion" (Legione SS Italiana). At present it would appear that two "SS" divisions exist in the territory of the Republic, made up as follows: - 1st Italian "SS" division (commander general Hansen with a Ist brigade of 5 battalions (commander colonel Diegitsch – sic: this was *SS-Oberführer* – since 20 April 1944 – Prof. Karl Diebitsch, born in Hannover on 3 January 1899, SS number 141 990) and a IInd brigade of 5 battalions, and a 2nd Italian "SS" division, probably made up of brigades named "Patria" (meaning homeland) and "Revere" (a hamlet of Borgo Mantovano in the Lombardy Province of Mantua in northern Italy, some 160 km and 30 km SE of the cities of Milan and Mantua respectively). According to other sources the two divisions are numbered the 18th and 30th. The "SS" battalions have generally been engaged in mopping-up operations, along with German "SS" units and in units no larger than a brigade". The "other sources" is in fact an anonymous typed chart headed "Order of Battle of the Republican Large Units" ("Quadro di battaglia delle G.U. Repubblicane") that appears to have been drawn up on information available upto 10 August 1944 that was not entirely correct. For example, while it is true that Himmler's original plan for the raising of Italian SS formations did envisage the creation of a second division six months after the first on the basis of the first's cadre ("*Programm für die Aufstellung der italienischen Miliz-Einheiten*", Nr. 35/143/43g, 2 October 1943), this never happened, and the only division to exist was numbered 29 and not 18 or 30. There is also no record of a brigade

named "Revere" (and why that name should have been used remains a mystery: assault brigades named "*Vendetta*", "*Patria*" and "*Italia*" were given in recruiting leaflets, but "Vendetta" was in fact another name for the "Degli Oddi" battalion, in April 1944 the Ist SS Battalion was called "Italia" (*I. SS-Btl. "Italia"*) and in February 1945 the IInd Battalion of SS Grenadier Regiment 81 was called "*Nettuno*" (*Battailon Nettuno II/G.R. 81 der SS*). The Italian "campi di concentramento" does translate literally as "concentration camps", but does not in this case have the same negative association as in other languages with the Holocaust and in fact refers to prisoner-of-war camps. Pinerolo is a town and municipality in the NW Province of Piedmont, some 31 miles (50 km) SW of Turin on the river Chisone.

(4) As reported in Dr. Marco Novarese's article "*Uniforms and Insignia of the Italian SS Legion*", page 11, "*Siegrunen*", Number 64, Fall 1997.

(5) *Der Reichsführter-SS, RF/M. 35/42/44, Feld-Kommandostelle, den 4. Mai 1944.* This was repeated in a secret telegramme sent on 14 May 1944 to the SS Economics and Administrative Head Office (*Wirtschafts-Verwaltungshauptamt*) in copy to the SS Main Operational Office (*SS-Führungshauptamt*) and Head Office of the Order Police (*Hauptamt der Ordnungspolizei*) in Berlin and the Highest SS and Police Leader in Italy in Verona by *SS-Oberführer* (promoted *SS-Brigadeführer und Generalmajor der Waffen-SS und Polizei* on 21 June 1944) Ernst Rode on behalf of the *Kommandostab-Reichsführer-SS.* Rode's message did not give any indication of the design of the collar patch. Since 25 April 1944, Rode (9 August 1894 – 12 September 1955) had been chief of staff to the commander of the so-called "band-fighting" (i.e. anti-partisan) units (*Chef des Stabes beim Chef der Bandenkampfverbände*), Erich von dem Bach (1 March 1899 – 8 March 1972).

(6) "*Verordnungsblatt der Waffen-SS*", 5th year of publication, number 8, Berlin, 15 April 1944, page 50, item 167. A Littorian fasces with its blade facing to the viewer's left is reported to have been used as the tactical symbol for vehicles of the Italian 29th SS Division, but no photographic evidence of this has so far been found (Schmitz/Thies: "*Die Truppenkennzeichen der Verbände und Einheiten der deutschen Wehrmacht und Waffen-SS und ihre Einsätze im Zweiten Weltkrieg 1939-1945*", *Band 2 Marine – Luftwaffe – Waffen-SS*", p. 458.

(7) "*SS Kalender 1945. Lommebog før danske SS-Frivillige*", published by the Germanic SS Battalions (*Germanske SS-Sturmbanne*), 1st year of publication, finished on 15 November 1944.

(8) "*Die Armschilde mit den völkischen Sinnbildern und die Kragenspiegel mit den politischen Sinnbildern der aussen- und nicht-deutschen Einheiten der Waffen-SS*", SS-Hauptamt, Amtsgruppe D, SS-Plannungstelle, 1 February 1945.

(9) The *Liktorenbundel* was shown by David Littlejohn as having been worn on both red and black patches, the colour change having been made in June 1944 ("*Foreign Legions of the Third Reich – Volume 2: Belgium, Great Britain, Holland, Italy and Spain*", R. James Bender Publishing, 1981, page 240). Collar patches credited to the collection of Frank Thayer were illustrated in the Addendum to Volume 2 on page 370 of Volume 4 in that same series published in 1987, both questionable and totally unconfirmed in contemporary photographs. Littlejohn's black and white illustration of the Liktorenbundel on red backing is reproduced on page 379 of Angolia's "Cloth Insignia of the SS" (Bender, 1983), and a photograph of an example on black is given on page 381. No mention is made of these collar patches in the Addendum to Angolia's book in the updated 2nd edition published in May 1989. The *Liktorenbundel* on a black patch is illustrated on page 20 of the article "*The Insignia and Organization of the Italian Volunteers to the Waffen-SS*" by Frank Thayer and Marco Pennisi ("*Military Advisor*", Bender, Fall 1996) and captioned "final pattern", as well as one of the same collar patches on a questionably "original" field jacket for an officer of the *29. Waffen-Grenadier-Division der Waffen-SS (italienische Nr. 1).* In the same article it is also stated (p. 18) that "*The RZM official collar tab, which features a machine-embroidered Lictorian bundle on black, does not appear to have been widely used. A metal insignia (sic) displaying three arrows over a rope circle with a scroll reading "ITALIA" was made by the Lorioli firm and was used on the black right-hand collar tab, apparently by members of the 1st Bn. of the 1st Regiment.*" This is incorrect insofar as the *Liktorenbundel* having been worn is concerned, and the "3 arrows" only having been worn by a single battalion. And the word "ITALIA" was on a yoke, not a scroll.

(10) Beadle and Davis did not show it in their ground-breaking "*Divisions Abzeichen der Waffen-SS Its Divisional Insignia*", Key Publications, Bromley, Kent, England which appeared in 1971, and illustrated the Liktorenbundel. Fosten and Marrion's "*Waffen-SS Its Uniforms, Insignia and Equipment 1938-1945*" for Almark was also published in 1971, stating on page 105 "The Roman fasces is alleged to have been worn but photographs show the SS runes". It would appear that the first time the "3 arrows" patch was illustrated was in 1981 on page 244 of Littlejohn's "*Foreign Legions of the Third Reich*", Vol. 2, Bender Publishing, which was captioned "Special collar patch said to be for the 1st Battalion of the 29th Division" and credited to the collection of the late Jim van Fleet of New Jersey. The identical image was reproduced on page 11 of Landwehr's "*Italian Volunteers of the Waffen-*

SS", *"Siegrunen"*, Glendale, Oregon, published 6 years later in 1987, with the qualification *"presumably II./WGR 81"*.

(11) The Sydney Rudolf Steiner College website gives the following explanation. "In 1924, Rudolf Steiner defined anthroposophy as *'... a path of knowledge, which intends to lead what is spiritual in the human being to what is spiritual in the universe'*. Anthroposophy is a source of spiritual knowledge and a practice as a path of inner development. Through Anthroposophy we can penetrate the mystery of our relationship with the spiritual world and seek answers and insights that are accessible through a schooling and development of one's inner life. It draws and builds on the spiritual research of Rudolf Steiner, who maintained that every human being (Anthropos) has the inherent wisdom (Sophia) to solve the riddles of existence and to transform as individuals as well as society. Anthroposophy is a spiritual philosophy and spiritual science that speaks to the deep questions of humanity, to our basic needs and the need to develop a relation to the world in complete freedom. It strives to develop not only natural scientific, but also spiritual scientific research and to bridge the divisions between the sciences, the arts and the spiritual strivings of man as the three main areas of human culture. Anthroposophy is also an impulse movement to nurture and honour the life of the soul in the individual and in society and is active in the world as applied or practical anthroposophy in various initiatives such as: Waldorf education, Biodynamic farming, Medicine, Curative education Eurythmy, The Christian Community, Architecture, etc. The term 'anthroposophy' predates Rudolf Steiner. The word 'anthroposophy' comes from the Greek (anthropos meaning 'human' and sophia meaning 'wisdom'). It can also be translated as 'wisdom of the human being' or understood as 'consciousness of one's humanity'. Anthroposophy is a spiritual philosophy; not a religion. It is a pathway to developing a conscious awareness of one's humanity. It recognises the inherent 'wisdom of the human being' to support a lifelong quest for spiritual self-development."

(12) *"Siegrunen"*, No. 64, Fall 1997, p. 11. Although Filippani-Ronconi in his pamphlet *"La 29a Divisione Granatieri SS"* Estratto da *"Arthos"* n. 7 n.s., Tipografia "Legoprint" – Genova", 2000, p. 6, refers to *"black collar patches, on which stood out the symbol of the three crossed arrows on a ring, as an alternative to the Siegrunen (of the) Waffen-SS"*, he makes no reference at all to the origins of such a symbol, let alone to anthroposophy.

(13) See, for example, *"Endzeitkämpfer Ideologie und Terror der SS"*, Deutscher Kunstverlag G.m.b.H., Berlin München, Kreismuseum Wewelsburg, p. 210.

(14) The translation of *"wollen, wissen and konnen"* as *"will, to know and to do"* is questionable, as in fact these words mean *"to surge (or wave), to know and to be able"*.

(15) Born on 11 March 1898, Tschimpke was awarded the Iron Cross 1st Class in World War I as a first lieutenant in the 157th Infantry Regiment. With NSDAP Party member 1 191 365, he joined the SS in 1932 with SS number 40 065 and was commissioned *SS-Untersturmführer* on 20 April 1933, then prior to WW2 was promoted to *SS-Obersturmführer* on 9 November 1933, *SS-Hauptsturmführer* on 18 March 1934, *SS-Sturmbannführer* on 9 November 1934, *SS-Obersturmbannführer* on 30 January 1936, and *SS-Standartenführer* on 30 January 1938. Success as a staff officer with the Southwest Upper District of the General SS (*SS-Oberascnitt Südwest*) in resolving problems of supply and logistics led Theodor Eicke in January 1938 to transfer Tschimpke to the Inspectorate of the SS Death's Head Units and Concentration Camps (*Stab SS-Totenkopfverbände und Konzentrationslager*) in Oranienburg. In October 1939, he joined what was then named the *SS-Totenkopf-Division* and on 12 June 1940 was awarded the 1939 Iron Cross 1st Class for his success as the T-Division's supply and transport officer (Ib) during the French campaign. In April 1941 Himmler appointed him to his operational staff (*Einsatzstab Reichsführers SS*), which was responsible for coordinating the activities of the infamous *Einsatzgruppen* and SD units in Russia. By 1942 he was on the staff of the *Reichsführer-SS* Heinrich Himmler (*Kdo.Stab RFSS*) and on 19 September 1942 was promoted to the highest rank he was to achieve, *SS-Oberführer,* and transferred to the Order Police (*Ordnungspolizei*) with the titular position of Police President of Chemnitz in the eastern German state of Saxony. In March 1943 Tschimpke was given an administrative position in Ukraine, where he was appointed as a district commissioner (*Gebietskommissar*) under Reich Commissioner (*Reickskommissar*) for Ukraine, Erich Koch (1897-1987). After the Germans were driven out of Ukraine by the Red Army in the spring of 1944, Himmler appointed Tschimpke as a special officer on the staff of the Highest SS and Police Leader in Italy, Karl Wolff, where he was involved with liaison with the RSI and the arming and training of the Italian SS. Rather curiously, given his talents and proven success in supply and logistics, he was put in charge of the Press and Propaganda Inspectorate (Ispettorato Stampa e Propaganda) of the Italian SS which had been formed on 11 March 1944. The last edition of the SS Officers' list (*Dienstaltersliste der Schutzstaffel der NSDAP*) updated to 9 November 1944 gave Tschimpke as serving in the SS Personnel Head Office (*SS-*

Pers.Hauptamt).

(16) Born 8 August 1896 in San Romano, Pisa Province, Mannelli joined the Fascist Militia (MVSN) on 1 February 1923 and in 1931 commanded its VIIth Anti-Aircraft Legion in Florence, in 1935 the IInd "Alpina" Legion in Turin and after promotion to Console Generale on 1 May 1939 was the Inspector General of the University Militia based in Rome from 28 October 1942 to 25 July 1943. He joined the *Waffen-SS* on 24 March 1944 with the rank of *Waffen-Brigadeführer und Generalmajor der Waffen-SS* and Inspector General of the Italian Armed Units of the SS.

(17) This number had been allocated on 26 November 1943 to the Headquarters of the Armed Militia (SS) – Kdo. Milizia Armata (SS), but on 5 September 1944 was changed to the Waffen-SS Commander in Italy (*Bef. d. Waffen-SS in Italien*): Kannapin, Volume III, page 37.

(18) *Der Höchste SS u.Pol.Führer "Italien" Der Befehlshaber der Waffen SS, Intendantur: Tgb.Nr. 644/44/CZ*, Oggetto Distintivi. The letter bore a stamp showing just "*Der Befehlshaber der Waffen-SS in Italien*". Scheriau was commissioned as an *SS-Untersturmführer* on 20 April 1937. His SS number was 275 505 and before the war he served in *SS-Standarte "Der Führer"*.

(19) The request was made by *SS-Hauptsturmführer* Scheriau in his letter (in Italian) to Lorioli dated 16 November 1944 under reference Prot.Nr. 711/44/Sche/Pa/B-2 and was date-stamped for receipt on 22 November 1944 under reference 16969. It read in literal translation: "*As for a parade of (Monday) 20 November 1944 there is need for at least 1500 badges, we ask you to provide at least that quantity by 19 November 1944 at the latest*". The "*parade*" in question would in fact appear to have been the ceremony held at Mariano Comense (Como) on Thursday, 23 November 1944, for the award of the Italian Silver Medal of Military Valour to the "*Degli Oddi*" Battalion (information kindly provided by Marco Novaresi via Fausto Sparacino, e-mail to the author, 31 March 2021). Despite the 3 working day postponement, the badges do not appear to have been delivered in time, as there is no trace of any of them being worn in any of the photographs taken of the ceremony.

(20) While Lorioli appear to have been the only Italian manufacture of metal badges for the Italian SS, another firm - VEDEME S.A. – received orders to manufacture items of cloth insignia, such as shoulder straps, collar patches and sleeve eagles. On 3 March 1944, for example, the Administrative Chief of the Headquarters Staff of the Italian Volunteer Legions *(Kdo.-Stab Ital.Freiw.Legionen, Der Leiter der Verwaltung)*, wrote to both Lorioli and VEDEME that the Italian volunteer Cesare Berardi would be visiting them to discuss orders for cloth and metal badges respectively.

(21) Filippani-Ronconi dismissed the theory that the "3 arrows" badge was only destined for use by the veterans of the Anzio Front, telling Novarese this was "completely wrong" ("Siegrunen", No. 64, Fall 1997, p. 10).

(22) Littlejohn, "*Foreign Legions of the Third Reich*", Vol. 2, Bender, 1981, p. 244.

(23) Littlejohn, op.cit., Vol. 4, Addendum to p. 244 of Vol. 2, R. James Bender Publishing, 1987. This identification is attributed to Col. Pier Amedeo Baldrati of Como, with whom Littlejohn is assumed to have corresponded. The author knew and corresponded with Baldrati during the 1960s and it is to be noted that he provided the insignia and flag illustrations for Pisanò's monumental work "*Gli Ultimi in Grigio Verde*", the 3-volume series originally published in monthly parts, subtitled "*Story of the Armed Forces of the RSI*", parts 29 and 30 of which were devoted to the Italian SS, but which made no reference to the "3 arrows" and in fact only illustrated the SS runes, on red and black patches.

(24) Novarese, "*Uniforms and Insignia of the Italian SS Legion*", in "*Siegrunen*", Number 64, Fall 1997, p. 10.

Bibliography

Massimiliano Afiero, "*Italiani nella Waffen-SS*", Associazione Culturale Ritterkreuz

Angolia, LTC (Ret.) John R.: "*Cloth Insignia of the SS*", R. James Bender Publishing

Avanguardia - Settimanale della Legione SS Italiana, third and final title, used from Anno I, N. 3 (01.04.44) - N. 42 (30.12.44) and from Anno II, N. 1 (06.01.45) to N. 16 (24.04.45)

Avanguardia - Settimanale illustrato per i volontari, second title, used only for Anno I, N. 2 (25.03.44)

Avanguardia Europea - Settimanale politico letterario, original title, used only for Anno I, N. 1 (18.03.44)

Beadle, C. & Hartmann, Theodor, "*Divisions Abzeichen der Waffen-SS its Divisional Insignia*", Key

Publications, Bromley, Kent, 1971, 130pp

Bortolotti, Giuliano: *"Non per guardarmi ma per ricordare. Memorie di un Volontario della Legione SS Italiana raccolte da Gabriele Ferrero"*, Libreria Bottazzi, Voghera, 2007

Corbatti, Sergio & Nava, Marco (pseudo.): *"Sentire – Pensare – Volere. Storia della Legione SS italiana"*, Ritter s.a.s., Milano, 2001

De Cecco, Victor. "*Waffen-SS Italiane*", 1980 (traduzione dal testo Tedesco Siegrunen)

Filippani-Ronconi, Pio: *"La 29ª Divisione Granatieri SS"*, Estratto da *"Arthos"* n. 7 n.s., Tipografia "Legoprint" – Genova, 2000

Kannapin, Norbert: *"Die deutsche Feldpostübersicht 1939-1945"*, Volume II, Numbers 41992 to 87919m Biblio Verlag, Osnabrück, 1982.

Landwehr, Richard, "*Italian Volunteers of the Waffen-SS*", Richard Landwehr, Siegrunen

Lazzero, Ricciotti, "*Le SS italiane*", Rizzoli, Milano, 1982

Lewis, Jim, "*Italian Volunteers in the Waffen-SS*", in the journal of the Third Reich Study Group, Vol. XIV, No. 3 (Whole No. 56), 1980, pp. 5-7

Littlejohn, David, *"Foreign Legions of the Third Reich. Vol. 2: Belgium, Great Britain, Holland, Italy and Spain"*, R. James Bender Publishing, San Jose, 1981

Littlejohn, David, "*Foreign Legions of the Third Reich. Vol. 4: Poland, the Ukraine, Bulgaria, Romania, Free India, Estonia, Latvia, Lithuania, Finland and Russia*" – Addendum to Volume 2 – Italy, R. James Bender Publishing, San Jose, 1987, pp. 367/371

Martelli, Capitano SS Leale, "*La SS Formazione Politico – Militare della Nuova Europa*", Tip. Cavalleri, Como, Aprile 1945-XXIII

Morandi, Carlo, "*A Noi!*", 1ª Edizione – Marzo 2013-XCI

Novarese, Dr. Marco & Turco, Cesare Benito, "*Italian Waffen-SS*", in "Siegrunen - *The Waffen-SS in Historical Perspective*", Richard Landwehr, Vol. X, No. 2, Whole No. 58, Spring 1995, pp. 35 - 43

Novarese, Dr. Marco, "*Italian Waffen-SS*", in "*Siegrunen - The Waffen-SS in Historical Perspective*", Richard Landwehr, Vol. X, No. 6, Whole No. 62, Fall 1996, pp. 27 - 37

Novarese, Marco, "*La Legione SS Italiana*" in Storia del XX Secolo, N. 31, 12/97 - pp. 20 - 26

Novarese, Dr. Marco: *"Uniforms and Insignia of the Italian SS Legion"*, Part I. of *"Italian Waffen-SS Section"*, in "Siegrunen", Number 64, Richard Landwehr, Fall 1997, pp.5/24

"Piccola Guida SS" a cura della Sezione principale Stampa e Propaganda Legione SS italiana, 1944-XXIII

Pisanò, Giorgio: *"Storia delle Forze Armate della R.S.I."*, "Documenti del nostro tempo", Edizioni F.P.E., Milan, Nos. 29 & 30, 6 and 13 September 1967 – published as chapters XXIX and XXX in *"Gli Ultimi in Grigio Verde. Storia delle Forze Armate della Repubblica Sociale Italiana"*, Edizioni F.P.E.

Ronconi, Guido, "*Les Waffen-SS allemands et italiens à la Bataille d'Anzio-Nettuno février-mai 1944 (1re partie)*", in "39/45 Magazine", No 137 – novembre 97, Editions Heimdal Sarl, Bayeux, pp 38/51

Ronconi, Guido, "*Die deutschen und italienischen Waffen-SS-Einheiten im Kampf bei Anzio-Nettuno (Februar - Mai 1944)*", in Der Freiwillige, Heft 3, 3/99, pp. 26 - 29

Sparacino, Fausto, "*Distintivi e Medaglie della R.S.I. 1943/45 della Legione SS Italiana dei Veterani della R.S.I.*", 2o Volume, E.M.I. – Serie "Militaria" 03, Milano, 1994

Taylor, Hugh Page, "*Recruiting Offices of the Italian SS in Italy (Uffici/centri d'arruolamento/di reclutamento – Werbestellen)*", in *"The Military Advisor"*, Volume 23, Number 2, Spring 2012, R. James Bender Publishing, San Jose, USA, pp. 2/11

Thayer, Frank, "*The Insignia & Organization of the Italian Volunteers to the Waffen-SS*", in *"The Military Advisor"*, Volume 7, Number 4, Fall 1996, R. James Bender Publishing. San Jose, USA

Vassalli, Giuseppe, "*Andenken. Ricordo. 29ª Division Grenadier Waffen SS*", Novantico Editrice, Pinerolo, 2012

TITOLI PUBBLICATI - ALREADY PUBLISHING

WW2 AXIS
FORCES

www.ingramcontent.com/pod-product-compliance
Ingram Content Group UK Ltd.
Pitfield, Milton Keynes, MK11 3LW, UK
UKHW061828190726
13853UKWH00009B/2486

9 788893 277761